Wainwright Family Walks

Volume 1:
The Southern Fells

Edited by
Tom Holman

FRANCES LINCOLN

Frances Lincoln Limited, 4 Torriano Mews, Torriano Avenue, London NW5 2RZ
www.franceslincoln.com

The Pictorial Guides to the Lakeland Fells published by Frances Lincoln 2003
This anthology first published by Frances Lincoln 2012

Publisher's Note

The fell pages in this book are taken from the Second Edition of A. Wainwright's
Pictorial Guides to the Lakeland Fells, comprehensively revised and updated by Chris
Jesty.

Please bear in mind that fellwalking can be dangerous, especially in wet, windy,
foggy or icy conditions. Be sure to take sensible precautions when out on the fells.
As Wainwright himself frequently wrote: use your common sense and watch
where you are putting your feet.

Printed and bound in China

A CIP catalogue record is available for this book from the British Library.

ISBN 978 0 7112 3362 1

9 8 7 6 5 4 3 2 1

Wainwright Family Walks
Volume 1: The Southern Fells

SYMBOLS
ON THE ROUTE MAPS

Route on motor road   Unenclosed ⌇⌇⌇⌇⌇
                              Enclosed ▰▰▰▰▰

Good footpath
(sufficiently distinct to be followed in mist)

Intermittent footpath
(difficult to follow in mist)

No path: route recommended   ············

(Off-route paths are shown in black.)

Wall   ∘∘∘∘∘∘∘∘∘∘∘∂   Broken wall   ∘∘∘∘∘∘∘∘∘∘∘ ∘

Fence   ++++++++++++   Broken fence   ''''''''''''''''''

Marshy ground   ⸜⸝⸜⸝⸜⸝   Trees   ⌀⌀⌀⌀⌀

Crags   ⋙⋘⋙   Scree   ⣿⣿⣿   Boulders   ⌀⌀⌀⌀

Stream or River   ⌇⌇⌇⌇⌇⌇⌇⌇⌇⌇⌇⌇⌇⌇➤
    (arrow indicates direction of flow)

Waterfall   ⌇⌇⌇⌇   Bridge   ⌇⫴

Buildings   ▰▰ ▪   Unenclosed road   ⁝⁝⁝⁝⁝⁝

Summit cairn   ▲   Other (prominent) cairns   △   △

Ordnance column   ▱   Limestone clints   ⊞⊞⊞⊞

Contours (at 100' intervals)   ···900···   Railway ═══

Miles from starting point   ④

Abbreviations:
O.S.: Ordnance Survey
Y.H.: Youth Hostel

Heights of fells, where stated in the book but not
confirmed by the Ordnance maps, are approximate

Contents

About Wainwright

The Lake District is well known for its literary history. Writers like William Wordsworth, Samuel Coleridge, John Ruskin and Beatrix Potter are forever linked to the Lakes and are the chief draw for thousands of visitors a year. All of them owe much of their creativity to this beautiful corner of the country, and all, in one way or another, express their attachment to it in their writing. But it is safe to say that no writer has chronicled the Lake District with as much affection and care, nor nearly so extensively, as Alfred Wainwright.

Like most of Cumbria's literary heroes, Wainwright was what locals call an off-comer. Born in Blackburn in 1907, he did not travel north to the Lake District until he was twenty-three, and like many people before and since, he was instantly entranced by what he saw – the open spaces, the fresh air, the pretty lakes and tarns and, above all, the majestic fells. He came back often after that, but it was not until his mid-thirties that he found the opportunity, via a job in the treasurer's office in Kendal, to settle in the area.

Another decade went by before Wainwright hit upon the idea that was to be his masterpiece – a complete study of the mountains of the Lake District. After breaking the area down into seven regions he identified 214 tops that he thought worthy of being called fells, and set himself a thirteen-year schedule to climb each and every one from every direction possible. At first he intended to record what he saw, in sketches and notes, for his own pleasure, but with the help of a local librarian and printer he was able to turn his first collection – his *Pictorial Guide to the Eastern Fells* – into a book. Sales took off, and the audience eagerly awaiting the next instalment grew with successive books.

Such a major survey of the Lake District is ambitious in itself, but it was the way Wainwright went about his task that made his *Pictorial Guides* so special. He prepared every page of his seven books by hand, each of them immaculately presented and ready for the printer's press without a scrap of type in sight. He wrote the books in his forties and fifties, all the time holding down a full-time job in Kendal, and his work was done with military precision, with weekends devoted to walking and weeknights dedicated to writing up his pages. Each book took nearly two years to prepare, and he finished the research for his last fell – Starling Dodd in the *Western Fells* – with a week to spare on his schedule. His *Pictorial Guides* are testament to his remarkable resolve and stamina, both out on the fells and at his desk, but they are much more than a simple directory of the mountains. Wainwright called the books his 'love letter' to the Lakes, and as well as being immensely practical companions they are full of opinion, humour and passion – an expert and exquisite series quite unlike anything else before or since.

It is now more than fifty years since the *Pictorial Guides* were launched, and the books have remained consistently popular and adored ever since. Wainwright wrote many more books about Cumbria and beyond before his death in 1991, and became a rather gruff television star for a while when his walks were filmed by the BBC. But it is his *Pictorial Guides* that are his greatest legacy, and it is proof of their timeless appeal that the books are as revered now as they ever have been. The 214 fells that he recorded have become something of a challenge for Wainwright fans and completists, and his work has inspired a host of spin-off merchandise and books – of which this is one.

About this Book

Wainwright usually walked in the fells alone, and did not have much time for stragglers. His reputation as a serious walker with unflagging stamina and a supremely methodical approach to his research has led many to think that his books are for hardened walkers only – people who stride up Helvellyn before breakfast and speed from top to top in full mountain gear.

But this image is unfair. Wainwright used his *Pictorial Guides* to show that there were fells and walks in the Lake District for everyone to enjoy, and he always appreciated the needs of slower walkers, young or old, even if he might not have cared for them to join him on his own walks. In his *Outlying Fells of Lakeland* book, compiled after the seven *Pictorial Guides* as what he called 'a mopping-up operation', he directly addressed the needs of walkers who were unable or unwilling to spend all day hiking across a multitude of tops. He had in mind those who, like himself, were getting a little too old for slogs up Scafell Pike or Great Gable, but he could just as well have been considering the needs of families. Walking in the Lake District is for all, he wrote in his introduction to the *Outlying Fells* book. 'Fellwalking is a pastime available to everyone, and unlike games and sports is not restricted to age groups. It is a pastime for the young and the middle-aged and the old.'

Because the *Outlying Fells* has so much to offer families, and because it has the southern half of the Lake District as its emphasis, many of the walks in this book are drawn from there. But it also borrows from Wainwright's *Pictorial Guides* to the 'proper' Lakeland fells which, as he often pointed out, had plenty of tops at relatively low level that bear favourable comparison with summits two or three times their height.

The purpose throughout this book is to recommend fells that are particularly suited to the needs of families. They have been chosen to provide a variety of starting points, with the emphasis on popular tourist towns and villages like Ambleside and Grasmere. They have a focus on the central area of the Lake District where many families like to stay, but also take in the less well-known fringes of the National Park, including those out towards the west coast. They include some of the most popular fells in the Lakes, like Helm Crag and Loughrigg Fell, but also some that are much less trodden, like Beacon Fell and Muncaster Fell. The most popular fells are usually so for good reasons, so don't let the crowds put you off, and head out to the further reaches of the Lake District if you want more space to yourself.

The book also takes in some key points in Wainwright's life, like Orrest Head, the fell he climbed on his first visit to the Lake District, and Scout Scar, a walk that starts from Kendal's town hall, his workplace of many years, as well as several of his personal favourites. There are walks that give tasters of the Lake District's grander fells, like Nab Scar on the Fairfield horseshoe and Stickle Pike, which forms part of a small horseshoe of its own in Dunnerdale, and walks that are ample targets in their own right, like Wansfell and Black Combe.

Families' walking abilities vary enormously, of course, according to the age and willingness of children, so there is a wide range of walks to choose from – from a mile-long stroll up Gummer's How to a challenging circuit of Harter Fell. The walks are arranged in rough order of difficulty, measured by a combination of distance, ascent and trickiness of terrain and wayfinding. The longest is seven and a half miles, and none of the fells except Harter Fell reaches more than 2,000 feet. Some, in fact, barely reach the height generally needed to be called a fell, and at least one, Finsthwaite Heights, is not a fell at all. But all twenty walks provide a flavour of what makes the Lake District unique and special, and prove Wainwright's theory, often repeated in his notes, that you do not always need to walk far or high to find spectacular summits and views. It also tries to provide a variety of terrain, taking in some of the best lakes, tarns and forests as well as fells.

Each walk in the book provides detailed directions for Wainwright's suggested route or – in cases where he provides more than one – the most suitable of them, plus information on how to get to the starting point and tips for family-friendly places to eat and things to do near by. The directions are detailed and prescriptive in order to give clear guidance to families on the fells, but the notes from Wainwright's books that accompany each walk often provide details of alternative ascents and descents for anyone who wishes to vary things.

The choice of walks is based on a variety of factors, not least among them Wainwright's own endorsements and opinions on the suitability of fells for less experienced fellwalkers. The all-important views-to-effort ratio is a key consideration, so the walks include plenty that provide outstanding panoramas of the Lake District for very little puff. So too is the quality of walking underfoot, which favours fells with good paths and easy wayfinding over those with more challenging slopes and stretches that are too steep, boggy or hard to follow.

All but a few of the walks are reachable via public transport. Linking up a fell to buses and trains requires careful advance planning and, sometimes, an extra walk, and public transport is not cheap in the Lake District – but then neither is car parking or petrol, and any efforts to reduce the number of cars on the roads are to be encouraged. Catching a bus or train also allows you to see much more of the Lakes than you will from behind a wheel, and if you try to make full use of it you will be in excellent company; while researching his books, Wainwright started and ended his walks on public transport, and claimed never to have missed a bus home throughout his research.

The book tries to take into account the needs of children, especially those for whom walking is not necessarily the first choice of activity. The walks avoid the worst of the fells' rock faces and precipices, and single out points of interest that will help to keep children motivated and moving. Walking in the Lake District can never be entirely without risk, and nor would most people want it to be, so there are some fells that might not be suitable for all children, and points of walks at which extra care is required; these are highlighted in the introductions and directions for each. Beyond this, the usual rules of safe fellwalking apply. Take a map and compass with you, and know how to use them, because even with detailed directions and Wainwright's sketches, it can be easy to take a wrong turn in the fells or find yourself in a blanket of mist. GPS devices can help too, but it is important to understand exactly how they work and accept their limitations. In the directions to these walks, grid references have been included at key points to help GPS and Ordnance Survey map users track their progress and identify where they should or shouldn't be. Make sure you take proper equipment with you into the fells, keep a close eye on the weather forecast and, in light of the first rule of the Lakeland climate – that whatever it is like as you set out, the conditions on the tops are often totally different – pack lots of layers, especially for children, and take supplies of food and drink. Parents should also go prepared to keep young walkers encouraged when the going gets tough; a bag of sweets and a head full of stories are just two of the essentials.

Beyond all these selection criteria this choice of walks is, like all collections, inevitably something of a personal one. Wainwright aficionados will doubtless be able to nominate many more fells that they consider worthy of inclusion here, and there are delightful parts of the Lake District, like Kentmere and Wasdale, that are not featured, usually because they do not have fell walks that are both suitable for families and worthy of a visit ahead of the rest. But that is not to say that these and other areas do not have anything to offer, and as children get older and more ambitious in their walking, there are countless more fells for families to try. Delve further into Wainwright's peerless *Pictorial Guides* and *Outlying Fells* to discover a lifetime's worth of walking – and in the meantime, I hope you enjoy these walks as much as my family and I have.

Tom Holman
Cumbria, January 2012

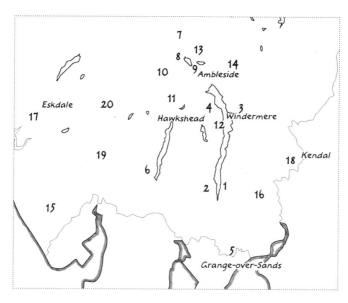

1 Gummer's How
2 Finsthwaite Heights
3 Orrest Head
4 Latterbarrow
5 Hampsfell
6 Beacon Fell
7 Helm Crag
8 Silver How
9 Loughrigg Fell
10 Lingmoor Fell

11 Holme Fell
12 Claife Heights
13 Nab Scar
14 Wansfell
15 Black Comb
16 Whitbarrow
17 Muncaster Fell
18 Scout Scar
19 Stickle Pike
20 Harter Fell

1 Gummer's How

from the Newby Bridge to Bowland Bridge road

Of all the Lake District fells so lovingly sketched and discussed by Alfred Wainwright, Gummer's How may well be the easiest. It is barely a fell at all, weighing in at only a shade over 1,000 feet (300m), and more than half of its ascent is taken care of by the drive to the starting point of this walk. The distance from car park to the summit is just ½ mile (800m), and the paths for most of the way are so well trodden that even small children will find little difficulty in getting to the top. As Wainwright notes, the route is so easy that directions are almost superfluous – 'If ... you get lost the future for you is bleak and without hope' – though they are included below to make quite sure no-one loses their way.

Given its simplicity, Gummer's How is a tremendous fell, with rewards far outstretching the effort required to climb it. Wainwright calls it 'a fellwalk in miniature', and within its short length it offers a taste of many of the best aspects of the Lakeland hills – soft grassy slopes to rest or picnic on, rocky outcrops to pick your way over, expanses of heather and hardy, windblown trees. The summit is a proper top too, with a fine old Ordnance Survey triangulation point rising out of the rocks, by or on which children can pose for photos, and mini rock faces near by for them to scramble over. It is a much more exciting place to be than many fells over twice its height, and its easy accessibility makes it ideal for any children who are reluctant to tackle more arduous ascents. Wainwright calls Gummer's How 'an old man's mountain' – but it is just as much one for families.

Above all, Gummer's How has outstanding views that make the final short clamber to the top completely worthwhile. The best aspect of the panorama is the view of the full, snaking length of Windermere, which at 10½ miles (17km) is by some distance the longest of the Lake District's eighteen lakes, and the boats making their way over it in all directions. Further north are the Coniston fells, while to the south is the vast expanse of Morecambe Bay.

The views from Gummer's How are tremendous at any time of the year, but they are particularly good on summer's evenings with the sun glistening on the lake or in the rich colours of autumn, and it also makes a good option on winter's days if higher fells are out of reach because of snow. If you visit in June, you may find yourself sharing the fell with fell runners, who compete in a race from Newby Bridge which involves a row across the lake and a lung-busting run up the hill from the bottom. Even if you don't meet the runners, you are likely to share the fell with others, as its accessibility makes it one of the most popular strolls in the southern Lake District – but don't let that put you off.

From *The Outlying Fells of Lakeland*

Distance 1 mile (1.6km)

Ascent 390 feet (120m)

Start and finish point The free Forestry Commission car park by Astley's Plantation on Fell Foot Brow – the road between Newby Bridge and Bowland Bridge (SD 389 876)

Ordnance Survey maps Explorer OL7; Landranger 96

Getting there
From either Newby Bridge or Windermere, take the A592. The turn-off is just under 1 mile (1.6km) from Newby Bridge, on the right when coming from this direction. After just under 1 mile (1.6km) of steep ascent, the car park, named after Gummer's How, is signposted on the right. It can fill up quite quickly on a warm summer's day; park carefully on the road either side of it if so.

With a bit of extra effort, it is possible to connect the walk with public transport. The 618 bus links Barrow-in-Furness to Ambleside via stops including Ulverston, Bowness, Windermere and Troutbeck Bridge, passing along the A592 and stopping at Fell Foot Park, close to the turn up Fell Foot Brow for the starting point. It is a slog of a walk up the road from here to the footpath for Gummer's How. The X35 bus stops at Newby Bridge, adding another mile (1.6km) on to the distance to walk in each direction. If you are getting off the bus here, avoid much of the A592 by walking up to Fell Foot Brow via Staveley.

Facilities, food and drink

A couple of miles further on from the car park towards Bowland Bridge is the Mason's Arms, a pub with terrific views of the Lyth Valley (015395 68486, www.masonsarmsstrawberrybank.co.uk). It serves excellent food and has cosy rooms with fires and a nice outdoor terrace. Children are welcome and have their own menu. A little further on from the pub in Bowland Bridge itself is the Hare and Hounds, another traditional Lakeland inn with good food and a nice garden with space for children to play (015395 68333, www.hareandhoundsbowlandbridge.co.uk). Both pubs have rooms to stay over. Opposite the Hare and Hounds is the Bowland Bridge Stores (015395 68643, www.bowlandbridgestores.co.uk), selling lots of local produce from which to make up a picnic.

There are more eating options in the hotels south of the walk at Newby Bridge. The best of them is the Swan (015395 31681, www.swanhotel.com), which has a restaurant, pub, side room with children's toys and books and a swimming pool inside, and outside tables overlooking the River Leven where it joins Windermere lake.

Many families combine a walk up to Gummer's How with a visit to Fell Foot Park, the National Trust-owned parkland by the bottom of Windermere (015395 31273, www.nationaltrust.org.uk). There are acres of grassy slopes to play or picnic on, plus a children's adventure playground, café and shallow spots for paddling in the water or boating. You can also catch a small shuttle boat to take you the short distance across the lake to Lakeside, which offers an aquarium (015395 30153, www.lakesaquarium.co.uk) and rides on the Windermere ferries (015394 43360, www.windermere-lakecruises.co.uk) or the Lakeside & Haverthwaite Railway (015395 31594, www. lakesiderailway.co.uk).

Directions

1 Leave the car park to the road and turn right up the hill. Take care on this stretch – it can get busy in the summer. After 165 yards (150m), cross and turn off the road to your left, through a gate by a footpath signposted for Gummer's How. The path ahead is perfectly clear, and is flat at first before rising via a series of stone steps which are good for scrambling children.

2 Where the steps run out by a fence corner and wooden footpath post, the path splits (SD 390 883). Carry on climbing via the middle fork for a short, rocky scramble, or take the left-hand one for a grassier ascent through the heather. The paths then become less distinct, but the way to the top is obvious and the summit's triangulation point (SD 391 885) soon comes into view. The very peak of Gummer's How is rocky, but there are plenty of grassy spots all around to enjoy the views and some refreshment. See Wainwright's notes for details of the fells you can see, and walk a little further on from the summit to see the full length of Windermere.

3 To return, either retrace your steps or, for variety, pick the grassy path that runs north-west of the summit. A wooden post after about 100 feet (30m) shows you are heading in the right direction. The path winds down and around the fell and returns you to the fence corner and wooden post reached earlier. Retrace your steps down the stony steps and flat path back to the road, and turn right at the gate for the car park.

Gummer's How
1054'
390 feet of ascent

from *THE NEWBY BRIDGE TO BOWLAND BRIDGE ROAD*

1 mile there and back
1 hour plus

The time comes to every Lakeland fellwalker, in due course, when he has good reason to give thanks to Gummer's How for salvaging his pride. Here is a fellwalk in miniature, a little beauty, with heather, a few rocks to scramble on, soft couches for repose, a classic view and a rustic Ordnance column — just like the real thing; and all so easy of access from a motor road and attainable almost without effort. White hair and Gummer's How are akin. It is an old man's mountain. And when ancient legs can no longer climb it know ye that the sad day has come to hang up the boots for ever and take to slippers.

MAP

No written description of the ascent is given.

Let this be a test of map reading, route finding and direction sense. If these abilities are so diminished that you get lost the future for you is bleak and without hope.

On the summit, take a path going northwest of the column (100 yards) for the best view of Windermere.

For an alternative route of return take the most easterly of the paths to the north.

The path up Gummer's How is part of a long-distance footpath, the Windermere Way, which encircles the lake.

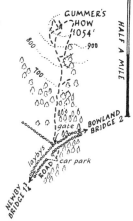

GUMMER'S HOW
1054'
HALF A MILE
800
900
700
gate
BOWLAND BRIDGE 2
laybys
ROAD
car park
NEWBY BRIDGE 1½

Gummer's How
from Lake Side

SWAN

19

THE VIEW

The diagram shows the major Lakeland fells in view from the summit. Additionally, to the east, the Howgills and the Pennine skyline can be seen. South is Morecambe Bay and the estuaries of the Kent and Crake.

The highlight of the panorama is the fine full-length prospect of Windermere, seen best from a vantage point northwest of the Ordnance column. Esthwaite Water also displays its full length but is greatly foreshortened by distance.

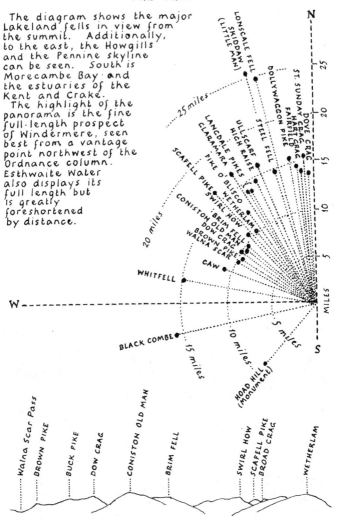

looking northwest to the Coniston Fells

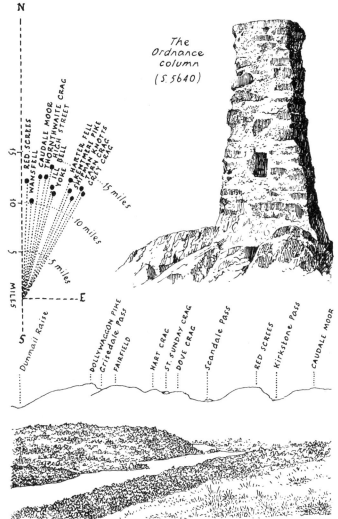

The Ordnance column
(S. 5640)

N

S

E

RED SCREES
WANSFELL
CAUDALE MOOR
THORNTHWAITE CRAG
ILL BELL
HIGH STREET
YOKE
HARTER FELL
KENTMERE PIKE
SHIPMAN KNOTTS
TARN CRAG
GREY CRAG

5 miles
10 miles
15 miles

5
10
15
MILES

Dunmail Raise

DOLLYWAGGON PIKE
Grisedale Pass
FAIRFIELD
HART CRAG
ST. SUNDAY CRAG
DOVE CRAG
Scandale Pass
RED SCREES
Kirkstone Pass
CAUDALE MOOR

looking north to the head of Windermere

21

2 Finsthwaite Heights
from Finsthwaite or Newby Bridge

Finsthwaite Heights is the only peak in this book that is not actually a proper fell. But it does provide a very pleasant family outing, and takes in a little climbing up to the two tarns above Finsthwaite – High and Low Dam. The pretty pools of water on shelves set into the slopes make for little summits in themselves, and are great places to rest or picnic. The much larger High Dam is also popular among hardy swimmers in the summer.

This walk provides two alternative starting points – Finsthwaite for a short, straightforward, up-and-down hike to the Dams; and Newby Bridge, for those who want to extend things by a couple of miles. The outward stretch of the longer walk passes through the woodland north of Newby Bridge, taking in a viewpoint at Waterside Knott and Finsthwaite Tower, sketched and described by Wainwright in his notes; while the return leg comes down a nice shallow valley and more woodland. Choose your route according to the time you have to spare and the walking abilities of your children; if you are starting from Finsthwaite, you need only follow steps 4 and 5 in these directions.

Either option provides a lovely stroll through the rolling hills and valleys of the southern Lake District, and a pleasant contrast to more rugged fells elsewhere. 'This is not fellwalking,' Wainwright admits in his notes – but it is delightful nevertheless.

From *The Outlying Fells of Lakeland*

Distance 2 miles (3km) or 4½ miles (7km)

Ascent 400 feet (120m) or 900 feet (275m)

Start and finish point The car park in front of St Peter's Church at Finsthwaite (SD 368 878) or the car parking spaces by the road junction at the Swan Hotel in Newby Bridge (SD 369 863)

Ordnance Survey maps Explorer OL7; Landranger 96

Getting there

If you are starting the walk at Finsthwaite, it is best reached via the A590 turn-off at Newby Bridge. There is plenty of parking in front of the church; leave a donation in the honesty box in the churchyard wall, and do not park here when there is a service on. There is more parking a little further on through the village, by an alternative way up to Low and High Dam.

Parking at Newby Bridge can be found just over the bridge from the A590, on the left-hand turn signposted for Finsthwaite and Rusland. The roadside parking spaces are immediately after the junction. You may also be able to park at the Swan if you visit before or after; tell hotel staff your plans.

Newby Bridge is served by the X35 bus running between Barrow-in-Furness and Kendal and the 618 from Barrow to Ambleside, which also stops at Windermere train station. Buses stop very close to the Swan Hotel off the A590. The only bus serving Finsthwaite is the 538, which runs on Thursdays only.

Facilities, food and drink

This walk is well situated for families, with lots to do near by. Hard by the alternative starting points at Finsthwaite and Newby Bridge respectively are the pretty St Peter's Church, usually left open for visitors; and the Swan Hotel, which has a pub, restaurant and swimming pool, plus a side room with children's toys and books (015395 31681, www.swanhotel.com).

Just beyond Finsthwaite is the Stott Park Bobbin Mill, an interesting old mill that produced the bobbins for Lancashire's once-vast spinning industry (015395 31087, www.english-heritage.org.uk/daysout/properties/stott-park-bobbin-mill; open from April to October). A mile (1.6km) from both Finsthwaite and Newby Bridge is Lakeside, which offers access to the Lakeside & Haverthwaite Railway (015395 31594, www.lakesiderailway.co.uk) and Windermere ferries (015394 43360, www.windermere-lakecruises.co.uk), both popular with families, and the Lakes Aquarium (015395 30153, www.lakesaquarium. co.uk). There is a café here too.

Directions

1 From the car parking spaces, walk back towards the Swan Hotel but turn left before you reach it up the road with brown signposts for Lakeside Steamers and the Stott Park Bobbin Mill. It soon crosses a bridge, and you may see a steam train from the Lakeside & Haverthwaite Railway puffing underneath. Immediately over the bridge, turn left on to a rougher road, signposted for Finsthwaite and Waterside Knott. After about 55 yards (50m), leave it to the right on a footpath, again signposted for Finsthwaite.

2 The path rises up some stone steps to a small wooden gate and a noticeboard introducing you to Waterside Knott. Carry on climbing up through the wood, and after picking up the moss-covered ruins of a dry stone wall to your left for a while, bend sharp right when the path meets some rocks. Rise again, over some more stone steps for a short stretch, to reach a wooden signpost indicating the way to a viewpoint. Follow it for good views, spoiled rather by the main road snaking through. There are rocks to perch on, but take care of children here as the drops are steep (SD 370 868).

3 Continue on the path from the viewpoint to pass through a gap in a wall and meet the main path again. Turn right along it, with Finsthwaite Tower soon coming into view ahead. Divert along a footpath marked by a signpost to walk around the tower, then take a path from the left of the tower to drop back down to the main path. At a signpost about 110 yards (100m) on from here, bear half right in the direction of the white arrow. The path drops down to reach a track through the wood; turn left along it. At a fork of paths keep to the broader left-hand one, then at another turn sharp left to reach a stile in a wall. Cross the field ahead to reach Finsthwaite, emerging at the village hall and church (SD 368 878).

4 From the church, take the narrow road between houses; it is the one directly ahead of you over the parking area. At a T-junction with a post-box turn right. After 30 yards (30m), leave the road to the left by a public footpath sign to cross a gravel drive to a wicket gate. Follow the direction of the yellow arrow to cross a field to another gate, then continue ahead on a broad track. After 20 yards (20m), leave it to the right, the way indicated by a yellow arrow and a hand-written sign for High Dam. The grassy path rises up to a kissing gate and footbridge, then joins the main path up to High Dam. Immediately after passing through another gate the path splits; take the left-hand fork, indicated by a yellow arrow. After 55 yards (50m) it splits again; this time take the path ahead, marked by a white arrow. It now rises up to the corner of Low Dam (SD 364 885).

5 Follow the path to the right of the water. Via two wooden footbridges it leads you up to High Dam. A clear path runs all the way around High Dam if you want to make a circuit of it, and it is a fine place to rest and picnic. Otherwise, turn left to take the path along the edge of High Dam. Ignore all side paths into the trees until just before a wooden footbridge, when a yellow arrow indicates the turn to take. The path weaves through the trees, passing through two small wooden gates – the second forking you away slightly – and returns you to the foot of Low Dam. Retrace your steps back to the church, taking care over the rocks if wet.

6 In front of the church, turn right down the road you came in on, but after 20 yards (20m) leave it to the right through an iron kissing gate, the way indicated by a signpost for Newby Bridge. Now cross a succession of fields, passing over four dry stone walls that cross your way, via a stile, gate, gap and ladder stile. Over the last, bear left on the path through the trees. At a fork of paths just over 110 yards (100m) on, bear left to follow the yellow arrow, and soon cross a gap in a broken wall. Drop down to leave the wood at a wooden gate and stile, which leads on to a track. Follow it down to the railway bridge crossed earlier and the car parking spaces.

Finsthwaite Heights

No definite summit.
Highest parts
about 570'.

900 feet of ascent

from NEWBY BRIDGE
4½ miles
3½ hours

Throughout this walk the scenery is sylvan with a few pastoral interludes. The only resemblance to fellwalking is in the ups and downs, but in this case the acclivities and declivities occur under foliage.

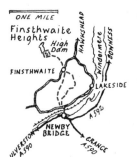

The walk as described is really two short outings combined and the quiet hamlet of Finsthwaite lies midway. The first section is the once-popular climb to the stone tower on the crest of the steep wooded hill at the foot of Windermere; the second part (which can be omitted but ought not to be) is a visit to the lovely Low and High Dams. Everywhere the surroundings are delightful. But this is not fellwalking.

26

Newby Bridge

Finsthwaite Church

Finsthwaite Tower

This memorial tower-cum-summerhouse is indicated on old 2½-inch Ordnance Survey maps as *Pennington Lodge Tower*. It is no longer kept in repair. A tablet high on the south wall is inscribed as follows:

ERECTED
TO HONOR THE
OFFICERS, SEAMEN AND MARINES
OF THE
ROYAL NAVY
WHOSE MATCHLESS CONDUCT AND
IRRESISTIBLE VALOUR DECISIVELY DEFEATED
THE FLEETS OF FRANCE, SPAIN AND HOLLAND
AND PRESERVED AND PROTECTED
LIBERTY AND COMMERCE
1799

Low Dam

High Dam

There is room to park beside the road to Rusland from the Swan Hotel. Go up the road on the west side of the hotel (signpost: Lakeside Steamers, Stott Park Bobbin Mill, etc.) and, over the railway bridge, turn left along an unmetalled road and then right (public footpath sign: Finsthwaite, etc.) up a flight of stone steps. Follow the path uphill through woodland for 300 yards and then turn sharp right. Another flight of steps assists progress at one point. Before long a post marks the start of a short detour to a viewpoint facing Newton Fell and Hampsfell. This detour is worth taking because the Tower has now no merit as a viewpoint, its former full-length and admirable prospect of Windermere being obscured by foliage. Bear left at the viewpoint, passing through a gap in an old wall, and rejoin the main path. At the top of the hill turn right at a post and left to Finsthwaite Tower. The entrance is walled up, but otherwise it is in a good condition. On the left-hand side of the tower a path will be found that leads back to the main path. In a hundred yards bear right at a post, and at the foot of the hill turn left at a T-junction onto a broad path through mixed woodland managed by the Woodland Trust. When the path forks bear left, and when a stile comes into view turn sharp left (or cut the corner off). On leaving the wood aim for the hamlet of Finsthwaite, which is visible ahead.

If the flesh is weak Finsthwaite is as far as one need go, returning to Newby Bridge by the alternative route shown on the map, to give an all-round trip of 3 miles. Those who are still strong enough to manage an extra 2 miles should bear left at the church along a narrow road and then right at a postbox. Leave the hamlet by a private-looking gate (signposted 'public footpath'), pass in front of cottages and up a ginnel (a narrow passage) to a wicket gate and cross a field to a similar wicket gate in its far top corner, there joining a cart-track curving left up a caravan-bespattered field. Leave the cart-track almost at once and continue on a rising grass path, due north, to a kissing gate and old wooden footbridge leading into a wood, where the broad path to Low Dam and High Dam* is joined and followed. Those who choose to may walk all the way around High Dam. Linger in the delectable surroundings here (it is a much nicer place than the over-populated Tarn Hows) before returning to Finsthwaite by first making a small detour around Low Dam (see map) and then rejoining the path of approach.

Back at the church, turn right through an iron kissing gate and follow a series of long pastures through a shallow valley, the right of way being indicated by four stiles. The last stile gives access to yet another woodland path. When this forks bear left, crossing a broken wall. On leaving the wood the path descends between gardens to a pleasant residential backwater and so back to the Swan Hotel.

*High Dam was constructed in 1835 to increase the area of Finsthwaite Tarn and to provide water and power for the Stott Park Bobbin Mill.

MAP

ONE MILE

RUSLAND

High Dam

Low Dam
gate
②

Finsthwaite
Heights

500

600

400

③

gate

car park

HAWKSHEAD

gate

300

gate

ROAD

Finsthwaite
✝ Church

gate

gate

RUSLAND

300

stile

LAKE SIDE

400

①

stile

HAWKSHEAD

500

stile

200

Lakeside

stile

stile

gate

600

stile

④

Tower

viewpoint

steps

400

ROAD

300

200

gate

railway

railway

Swan
Hotel

Leven

RUSLAND

River

ULVERSTON
A590

Newby
Bridge

BOWNESS
KENDAL
A592

GRANGE
LANCASTER
A590

Lakeside is the terminus of the steam railway to Haverthwaite and of the lake cruises to Bowness and Ambleside. Adjoining the termini is the Lakes Aquarium, where there are many kinds of creature other than fish. Half a mile beyond the aquarium is the Stott Park Bobbin Mill, which is open to the public from April to October, and a mile southwest of Newby Bridge is the Lakeland Motor Museum, which was moved here from Holker Hall in 2010.

3 Orrest Head
from Windermere

Orrest Head is the first taste of the Lake District for many people – Alfred Wainwright among them. It was to here, on 7 June 1930, that Wainwright came with his cousin from Blackburn, and the beauty of the scene captivated him immediately. 'It was a moment of magic, a revelation so unexpected that I stood transfixed, unable to believe my eyes,' he recalled. 'I saw mountain ranges, one after another, the nearer starkly etched, those beyond fading into the blue distance. Rich woodlands, emerald pastures and the shimmering water of the lake below added to a pageant of loveliness, a glorious panorama that held me enthralled. I had seen landscapes of rural beauty pictured in the local art gallery, but here was no painted canvas; this was real. This was truth. God was in his heaven that day and I a humble worshipper.'

Would Wainwright have formed such an attachment to the Lake District if his first climb had been less successful? Possibly, but Orrest Head certainly confirmed that the fells were where he wanted to be. The contrast with his industrial home town must have been startling, and the walk prompted him to return again and again from Blackburn, later for good. More than eight decades on, Orrest Head is renowned as the fell where Wainwright 'came in' to the Lake District, and a plaque on its top records the fact.

Partly because of the association with Wainwright, the fell can get busy, and the crowds and the traffic on the roads around Windermere now mean it is a less idyllic place than it was in 1930. But the panoramic scene from the top has changed little, and even if they are not quite the 'unrivalled views' of the fells promised by the board that marks the way up from Windermere, they are certainly far-reaching and splendid.

For most people, the walk to the top from Windermere is not quite the 20 minutes ambitiously advertised by the board either. But it is nonetheless very easy, making Orrest Head an ideal climb for families as well as beginners and those whose fellwalking glory days are behind them. Most children should be able to follow this route up and down within a couple of hours, and if they are flagging by the top there is the option of shortening the walk by simply returning by the way you came. But the return, leaving the fell to the north and returning via much quieter lanes and paths, makes a nice peaceful contrast to the flow of walkers climbing up from Windermere. The paths throughout are very easy, and the summit is a good spot for young walkers, with plenty of grassy areas for picnics and benches from which to enjoy the views.

From *The Outlying Fells of Lakeland*

Distance 2½ miles (4km)

Ascent 400 feet (120m)

Start and finish point Windermere train station (SD 414 986)

Ordnance Survey maps Explorer OL7; Landranger 90 and 96

Getting there

Windermere station is one end of the single-track branch line, sometimes called the Lakes Line, that connects Oxenholme on the west coast main line, plus Kendal, Burneside and Staveley. There are trains every hour or so, and less frequent direct services to Manchester. The station was much larger in the heyday of the railways, with four platforms and many more services, but it was pruned back to its current single platform in the 1970s and 1980s.

The train station is well served by buses – and this is how Wainwright first arrived in Windermere from Blackburn. The 555 bus stops on its way from Kendal to Keswick, while the 599 links the station to Bowness and Ambleside. The less frequent 618 brings you in from Barrow-in-Furness and other towns to the west, including Ulverston and Newby Bridge, and the 505 from Coniston and Hawkshead and the 516 from Langdale villages both extend to Windermere on Sundays. The 597 service ferries people around the town of Windermere itself.

If you are driving in, the train station is at the north end of Windermere, just off the A591 that runs across the north tip of the town. There is very limited parking in front of the station, and a much larger pay-and-display car park at the adjacent Booths supermarket, plus more spaces elsewhere in town.

Facilities, food and drink

There are plenty of places to find food and drink in Windermere. Right next to the station, Booths (015394 46114, www.booths.co.uk) is a particularly good place to stock up with a picnic for the top of Orrest Head, and there are several other cafés on the short stroll down into town that will make up sandwiches for the walk; Renoir's Coffee Shop (015394 44863) is particularly recommended. The large Lakeland shop near the station (015394 882000, www.lakeland.co.uk) also does very good lunches in its upstairs café.

Pub and restaurant-wise, the Lamplighter on the High Street (015394 43457, www.lamplighterdiningrooms.com) and the Grey Walls Inn on Elleray Road (015394 43741, www.thegreywalls. co.uk) do good food and welcome children. Most of the larger hotels in Windermere also have bars and restaurants.

There are plenty of family-friendly options for activities before or after a walk up Orrest Head. Many families head down to Bowness for a ride over the lake on one of the several ferries that serve the shore (015394 43360, www.windermere-lakecruises. co.uk). Bowness also has the World of Beatrix Potter, which Peter Rabbit fans will love (015394 88444, www.hop-skip-jump.com). You can hire bikes from Country Lanes on the Windermere station precinct (015394 44544, www.countrylaneslakedistrict. co.uk) and there are outdoor and indoor children's playgrounds and a café at the Lake District Visitor Centre at Brockhole, a couple of miles up the A591 towards Ambleside (015394 46601, www.brockhole.co.uk). Brockhole is also a good starting point for researching other visitor attractions in Windermere and beyond, as is the tourist information centre very close to the railway station on Victoria Street (015394 46499).

Directions

1 Turn left out of the station to the busy junction at the head of Windermere town. Carefully cross the road to your right towards the Windermere Hotel, then turn left. At the next junction you will see ahead of you the long-standing wooden sign for Orrest Head. Follow this quiet road as it climbs steadily up in loops, ignoring all side paths.

2 The tarmac path later gives way to a rougher track and splits into two. Take the right-hand path that climbs alongside a wall. At a T-junction, turn right on to a fenced path. Pass through a metal gate by a memorial tablet, given for the man who donated Orrest Head for public use. From here, it is a very short further climb to the summit (SD 414 994).

3 As Wainwright suggests, you can retrace your steps from here back to Windermere for a simple 1-mile (1.6km) stroll. If you want to extend things a little, head north from the summit, almost directly opposite the path you climbed, to pick up a grassy path. The background hum of Windermere traffic disappears as soon as you are off the top. The path drops down to a gate and wall stile by a footpath sign. Cross the stile and continue on across the fields until you reach a wall stile and gate (NY 417 000).

4 Cross and turn left on to the quiet road, soon passing a farm. The road continues pleasantly down to the busy A592, but a few steps before the junction, pass through a metal gate on your left to pick up a clear footpath. Continue past side paths and a track to enter a wood by a gate. Again ignoring all side paths, continue along the path, mostly under cover of trees, until you reach a road by Elleray Bank. Turn right down this, but almost immediately turn off left again by a wooden footpath post to pick up the path again. It leads you out to the lane up to Orrest Head used earlier. Turn right down it back to Windermere.

Orrest Head

783'
400 feet of ascent

from WINDERMERE
RAILWAY STATION
2½ miles
2 hours
by the route described

1 mile : 1 hour
there and back direct

from the north

Orrest Head, for many of us, is "where we came in" — our first ascent in Lakeland, our first sight of mountains in tumultuous array across glittering waters, our awakening to beauty.   It is a popular walk, deservedly, for here the promised land is seen in all its glory. It is a fitting finale, too, to a life made happy by fellwandering.   Dare we hope there will be another Orrest Head over the threshold of the next heaven?

The way to Orrest Head is announced by a large signboard, which proclaims its unrivalled views and states that it is a twenty minutes' walk to the top. It is the leftmost of three drives that leave the main road opposite the bank close to the railway station, and is a tarmac strip initially. Almost at once a footpath goes off to the left: ignore this, keeping ahead and climbing gradually in a series of loops and bends. When a smithy is reached the path becomes rough; further, it divides into three branches: take the one on the right by a wall to reach and enter a fenced lane with many seats. This leads to a kissing gate; in the wall alongside is a memorial tablet to Arthur Henry Heywood, whose family gave Orrest Head for public enjoyment. Through the gate, and clear of trees at last, the view-indicator on the summit is seen on the left and soon reached. There is a choice of seats — iron, wood, stone and grass — from which to admire the fine view and reflect that, once upon a time, you too could have done this climb in twenty minutes just like that signboard said. Never mind. You've had a good innings.

Return the same way, or, if a longer alternative route is preferred, leave the rocky top by a path heading north to a quiet byroad, which follow left to join the A592 road (to Troutbeck) but without actually setting foot on it go through a gate on the left (public footpath sign), whence a good path leads forward into a wood and continues very pleasantly past some handsome residences amid noble trees, rejoining the outward route only a few paces from the starting point: in fact along the path ignored earlier.

MAP

The view indicator on the summit

The indicator was replaced in 2002 and shows the view from Coniston Old Man to Harrison Stickle. It includes information about the area and records the fact that this is where the author first set foot in the Lake District.

THE VIEW

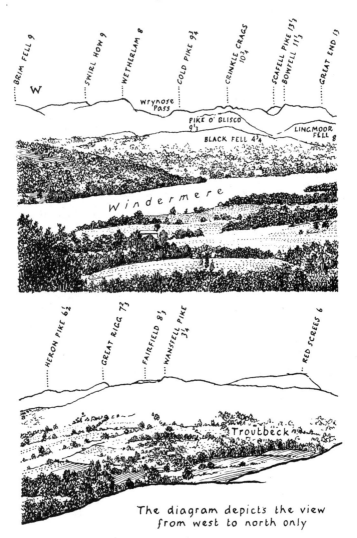

W

BRIM FELL 9
SWIRL HOW 9
WETHERLAM 8
COLD PIKE 9¾
CRINKLE CRAGS 10¼
SCAFELL PIKE 13½
BOWFELL 11½
GREAT END 13

Wrynose Pass

PIKE O' BLISCO 9⅓

LINGMOOR FELL 8

BLACK FELL 4¾

Windermere

HERON PIKE 6½
GREAT RIGG 7⅓
FAIRFIELD 8⅓
WANSFELL PIKE 3¼
RED SCREES 6

Troutbeck

The diagram depicts the view
from west to north only

THE VIEW

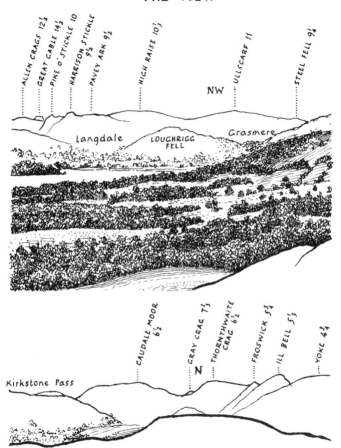

ALLEN CRAGS 12½
GREAT GABLE 14½
PIKE O'STICKLE 10
HARRISON STICKLE 9½
PAVEY ARK 9½
HIGH RAISE 10½
NW
ULLSCARF 11
STEEL FELL 9¼

Langdale   LOUGHRIGG FELL   Grasmere

CAUDALE MOOR 6½
GRAY CRAG 7¾
THORNTHWAITE CRAG 6½
FROSWICK 5¾
ILL BELL 5⅓
YOKE 4¾

N

Kirkstone Pass

The thick line is the outline of the summit rocks.

The figures accompanying the names of fells
indicate distances in miles.

Summit seats and litter, which occur in profusion,
and the view indicator, are omitted.

4 Latterbarrow
from Hawkshead

A good walk deserves a good summit with a good cairn perched on top – and there are few grander ones than Latterbarrow's. Stretching about 15 feet into the sky in three layers from the rocks on the top, this neatly constructed chimney-like obelisk bears testament to the skills of the Lake District's dry stone wallers and cairn builders, and can be seen from miles around – meaning that many people see Latterbarrow well before they actually climb it.

The size of the cairn is quite out of keeping with the fell itself, which reaches a height of barely 800 feet (240m) and is easily climbed, but it makes it a place that children enjoy reaching and remember. There are superb views in all directions too, including Lake Windermere, the Coniston fells, the Fairfield horseshoe and the Langdale Pikes, and it is a lovely spot to picnic on a warm day, though not a place to linger on a cold one. Like many fells, Latterbarrow takes its name from the Old Norse language, in this case meaning the hill where animals have their lair.

This walk extends Wainwright's suggested route slightly to start from Hawkshead, which offers plenty of parking and places for families to eat and visit. Latterbarrow is probably the most popular fell walk from the picture postcard village which, despite the influx of visitors most of the year round, is well worth exploring before or after. Its higgledy-piggledy houses and squares are delightful, and were walked by both William Wordsworth and Beatrix Potter, both of whom have close associations with the area. Like Latterbarrow, much of the village is looked after by the National Trust, which by and large does a good job of balancing the needs of nature, residents and visitors. The way up to the fell is via the hamlet of Colthouse and the plantations to its east, which have undergone much felling, while the descent is on Latterbarrow's west slopes and a quiet roadside back down to the village. Most of the walking is easy, though stretches over felled parts of the plantation and the drop down from the summit require a little care, and most families will manage the walk in a few hours.

From *The Outlying Fells of Lakeland*

Distance 3½ miles (5.6km)

Ascent 500 feet (150m)

Start and finish point The large Lake District National Park Authority pay-and-display car park on the edge of Hawkshead (SD 353 980)

Ordnance Survey maps Explorer OL6; Landranger 96

Getting there

Hawkshead is on the B5285, mid-way between Coniston and the western shores of Windermere lake. It is best reached by car via Ambleside from the north, Coniston from the west and Newby Bridge from the south. From anywhere east, you may prefer to take the car ferry that links Bowness with Far Sawrey on the other side of the lake, as it saves a long drive around the water's edge. It runs every 20 minutes from around 7am on weekdays (9am on Sundays, and nearer 10am in winter), though you may have to wait a while in high season as it carries only eighteen cars at a time. The ferry doesn't run in bad weather, so check in advance before you plan a journey (01228 227653). It carries pedestrians and cyclists as well as cars. From the Ferry House terminus near Far Sawrey it is about 3 miles (5km) on to Hawkshead. The car park there, like many in the Lake District now, accepts payment by credit card – which is just as well considering how much parking costs.

Hawkshead is served by the 505 bus that links Coniston and Ambleside. From early April to late October, a minibus service (number 525) connects Hawkshead to Ferry House via Far Sawrey about ten times a day, so it is easy to plan a journey from Bowness via ferry and bus. It may also be possible to take the X30 to and from the Ferry House, Far and Near Sawrey and Grizedale, though services are limited so check details in advance (0871 200 2233, www.traveline.info).

Facilities, food and drink

Hawkshead's large car park has public toilets, and a tourist information centre can be found just over the road (015394 36946, www.hawksheadtouristinfo.org.uk).

The village has plenty of options for eating and drinking. The Honeypot shop on the square is the perfect place to stock up on a picnic and sells lots of local specialities like Kendal mint cake, rum butter and fudge (015394 36267, www.honeypotfoods. co.uk). Across the square is the Kings Arms, a fine traditional Lakeland inn, with good pub food, beer and rooms (015394 36372, www.kingsarmshawkshead.co.uk). Other recommended pubs include the Queens Head (015394 36271, www. queensheadhotel.co.uk), while a little way out of the village in Outgate and Barngates respectively are the Outgate Inn (015394 36413, www.outgateinn.co.uk) and foodie Drunken Duck Inn (015394 36347, www.drunkenduckinn.co.uk).

Hawkshead also has a children's playground and a pretty church, St Michael and All Angels, which is perched on the hill above the village and left open for visitors. William Wordsworth attended the village's grammar school, and while it closed over a century ago you can still visit it and read the messages scratched by errant pupils on the desks (015394 36735, www. hawksheadgrammar.org.uk). Hawkshead was also frequently visited by Beatrix Potter, and her husband, William Heelis, had an office on Main Street that now houses the Beatrix Potter Gallery (015394 36335, www.nationaltrust.org.uk/beatrixpotter). A short drive away in Near Sawrey is Potter's house, Hill Top, which hosts popular tours (015394 36269). Another popular family destination near by is Grizedale Forest, which has play areas, a zip-wire adventure zone and a café as well as good walks (01229 860010, www.forestry.gov.uk/grizedale).

Directions

1 Leave the car park with your back to the village and walk along the road to a T-junction. Turn right. At the next T-junction turn left, following the signpost for Sawrey and Windermere. Cross a bridge, then turn off to the left on to a quieter road, this time signposted for Wray and Wray Castle. Walk up the road, ignoring side roads to the right, and pass a cluster of houses in Colthouse. After climbing more steeply, reach Cragg Cottage and, just past it, pass through a gate to the right that joins a clear, stony path (SD 359 986).

2 This path now climbs steadily, passing through three gates and, to your left, an area of the Colthouse plantation that has been substantially felled. At the very end of this area, where the fence on your right runs out and by a marker post, turn left on to a footpath. The path dips down then climbs again, via steps, to a gap in a wall. Continue on from this, the summit of Latterbarrow soon coming into view to your half left, before dipping down again and bending left. The path continues to wind, at first through more felled plantation and then woodland, and reaches a stile. Cross it and follow the clear path through the bracken to the towering obelisk on the top of Latterbarrow (SD 367 991). There are grassy spots and rocks to perch on to enjoy the views, and the monument provides some shelter from the wind if you need it.

3 From the direction you came, bear left to pick up a path down from the summit. It is steep at first, so take care, especially in the wet. If you are in any doubt, the direction you need is due west. The path descends on mostly grassy slopes through bracken and woodland to a wooden gate that leads on to the quiet Wray road, further up from the stretch followed earlier. Turn left and follow this road back to Colthouse, from where you can retrace your steps to Hawkshead. For an alternative route back to the village, turn right soon after emerging at the road and follow that road back via Hawkshead Hill, or leave it on the second footpath on your left back to Hawkshead.

Latterbarrow
803'
500 feet of ascent

from COLTHOUSE
2¾ miles
2 hours

from Hawkshead

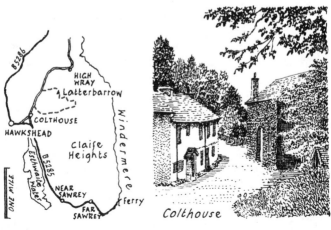

Colthouse

The lily tarn,
Colthouse Heights

Latterbarrow is well known by sight, if not by name, its elegant obelisk being prominently in view from Hawkshead and the Ambleside district. This bare hill, National Trust property, has been spared the forest encroachments from which so much of the west side of Windermere has suffered, and has a deserved reputation as a viewpoint. It is reached by a popular path leaving the Colthouse-Wray road or by a bridleway and a new forest track direct from Colthouse. These two approaches, if linked together, give a circular walk needing little effort yet yielding much delight.

The summit of Latterbarrow,
looking northeast

RED SCREES CAUDALE MOOR WANSFELL PIKE THORNTHWAITE CRAG HIGH STREET FROSWICK ILL BELL

The highlight of the walk is the summit of Latterbarrow and it is worth saving until the end. Therefore preferably do the walk anti-clockwise. There is space to park a car (one only) on the roadside near the Latterbarrow gate; if this is used start by walking down the road, south, for a third of a mile to a gate on the left opposite the end of a drive and identifiable by a huge yew near the track leading off. If parked at Colthouse, or coming on foot from Hawkshead, go up the Wray road to this point: it is just beyond Cragg Cottage on the right. Miles on the map below are measured from the Latterbarrow gate.

The track past the yew is a public bridleway leading distinctly up the wooded hillside and passing a lily tarn and many noble trees, mainly larch, to an area on the left where the trees have been felled. At the end of this area take a path on the left opposite a signpost. In 200 yards the path bends left up a flight of steps to a gap in the wall ahead. Then it continues, with many changes of direction, through felled areas and woodland, to a stile. From here a path leads up to the monument on the bare top of Latterbarrow. This is a fine viewpoint commanding a panorama of south-east Lakeland, with a mountain skyline ranging from the Coniston Fells to the Ill Bell range above the Brathay and Rothay valleys. Descend by either of the paths to the west and so reach the road and the parked car, or go left down to Colthouse.

MAP

The obelisk on the summit of Latterbarrow is known as Latterbarrow Man.

ONE MILE

The lily tarn is, after the manner of its kind, gradually growing smaller as vegetation encroaches from the banks. If left to its own devices it will eventually disappear.

46

5 Hampsfell
from Grange-over-Sands

Hampsfell is 'a hill small and unpretentious, yet endowed with an air of freedom and space,' wrote Wainwright in his notes. 'It is a place for looking northwards, indulging memories, and dreaming.'

Like many in this book, the walk is drawn from Wainwright's *Outlying Fells of Lakeland*, written 'primarily for old age pensioners and others who can no longer climb high fells but can still, within reason, potter about on the short and easy slopes and summits of the foothills.' This is an archetypal walk from that book – an easy enough climb to be within reach of most, but enough of one to make the rest on the top a just reward for your efforts.

The walk starts and finishes in Grange-over-Sands, a popular retirement town for those ex-fellwalkers for whom Wainwright was writing, but also a favourite of families visiting for the day or longer – though there are many days when you might not recognise his description of it as having 'a mild climate... and sunny location.' But the way up is suitable for older and younger walkers alike, and has varied terrain that children will enjoy including grassy slopes to run up and down and broad limestone pavements for a bit of easy scrambling at the top.

The summit of Hampsfell is marked by a square stone building – the Hospice, built by a vicar of Cartmel in the 1830s and still, as then, a welcome place for shelter from the rain – and there is plenty of flat space all around it to stretch out with a picnic, as well as wind-bent trees, wild flowers and often butterflies. Wainwright provides notes on the history of the hospice and the extensive messages on the walls inside, as well as a guide to the great views, which on a clear day stretch out to the higher fells to the north and across Morecambe Bay to the south. The way down from Hampsfell takes you back into Grange-over-Sands a different way, via the edge of Eggerslack Wood.

This walk is unlikely to take much more than a couple of hours even at a very leisurely pace. It can be cut further if you have someone able to drop you at the top of Grange Fell Road, or take the 532 bus towards Cartmel to deposit you there. If the distance is not enough and you feel like stretching your legs further, there are several other paths from the top of Hampsfell to take you onwards. Bearing north-west leads you down into Lindale, from where there are footpaths and buses back to Grange-over-Sands, while passing close to the top of the fell is the Cistercian Way, a 33-mile (55km) trail that hugs the peninsula from Grange-over-Sands to Roa Island in Barrow-in-Furness. That is probably a walk too far, but rather shorter is the stretch to Cartmel, which has a fine Priory and several pubs and cafés.

From *The Outlying Fells of Lakeland*

Distance 3½ miles (5.6km)

Ascent 700 feet (215m)

Start and finish point The pay-and-display car park on Hampsfell Road in Grange-over-Sands (SD 407 781)

Ordnance Survey maps Explorer OL7; Landranger 96

Getting there
Grange-over-Sands is on the B5277, off the A590. For the car park, follow the B5277 up to the crossroads by the public library and turn right. There are several more car parks in the town that are a short walk from Hampsfell Road, but the library car park near the start of the walk is for users only, and most of the street parking is limited to one hour only.

Grange is well served by trains and buses. The Furness Line from Lancaster and Manchester to Barrow stops here, and the final stretch of the journey across the sands is one of the very best in Cumbria. The X35 bus will get you to Grange station from Kendal, while the 532 bus connects Grange with Cartmel. To get to the start of the walk from the station, turn left to follow the path through the ornamental gardens, then turn right to leave it towards the shops. Follow the road uphill, past the clock tower and post office, until you reach the crossroads by the public library.

Facilities, food and drink

As befits its gentle Edwardian elegance, Grange-over-Sands has plenty of pleasant tearooms offering refreshment before or after a walk. The Hazelmere Café and Bakery on Yewbarrow Terrace, close to the station and the promenade, is particularly good (015395 32972, www.hazelmerecafe.co.uk). Recently named the country's top tea place by the Tea Guild, it has a mindboggling range of teas from around the world, plus home-made cakes and light meals. It is very child-friendly.

If you want some food for the walk, head for Higginsons Butchers on Main Street, a few metres from the library at the start of the walk (015395 35864, www.higginsonsofgrange. co.uk). It has excellent pies and a takeaway shop just round the corner that is perfect for putting together a picnic spread. There are small branches of Spar and Co-op very close by for further provisions.

For pubs, a short drive to Lindale provides the Lindale Inn (015395 32416) and the Royal Oak (015395 32882), and Cartmel in the other direction has several excellent ones to choose from. There are public toilets on the short walk between the car park and the library at the start of the walk, and if you need advice on accommodation or other activities in Grange-over-Sands, there is a tourist information centre on Main Street (015395 34026).

Directions

1 Leave the car park to follow the road into town, and turn right at the crossroads up Grange Fell Road, past the public library. Climb steeply up Grange Fell Road for about ¾ mile (1.2km).

2 Where the houses give way to fields on the right hand side, the pavement runs out. Take care along the road for the next 275 yards (250m) until you reach a wall stile on the brow of the hill on the right, marked by a public footpath sign for Hampsfell. Cross the field to another wall stile, and cross the farm road to a third one. Cross and turn right on to the footpath, guided by the wooden posts and, when you reach a junction with a broader path, turn left on to it. This path now climbs gently to a wall stile by a metal gate (SD 395 785).

3 Cross and take the half right path of two. From the brow of the next rise you will be able to see the square-shaped hospice among the trees on the horizon. The path leads directly up to the summit (SD 399 794), the last part over limestone slabs after crossing another wall stile. The chains around the hospice are only to keep out animals, and walkers are welcome to take shelter here. The building and the grassy top around are both ideal for a picnic. Take care climbing the stone steps to the roof of the building for fine views, identified by a board of fells as well as Wainwright's notes.

4 Take the path east from the hospice, soon reaching the corner of a dry stone wall. (If you need help finding your direction, use the giant compass on the hospice roof; when you are stood at the 90° mark, the way you need is straight ahead of you.) With the wall on your left, descend further to a small wooden gate that leads on to an old cart track on the edge of Eggerslack Wood. Turn right along it, soon passing through a large gate, and follow the track down. At a T-junction with farm buildings to the right, turn left through a gate and down the track again. It soon becomes a quiet road, Hampsfell Road, that winds pleasantly down towards Grange-over-Sands and the car park.

Hampsfell
727'
700 feet of ascent

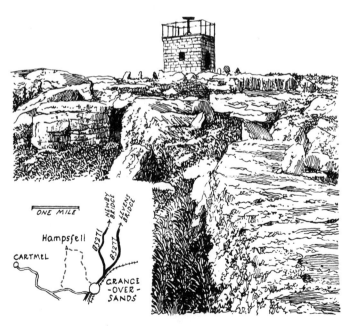

from GRANGE-OVER-SANDS
(CLOCK TOWER)

3½ miles
2 hours

Hampsfell is the name commonly used on signposts and by the local people; it was formerly recorded on Ordnance maps as *Hampsfield Fell* (of which 'Hampsfell' is probably a corruption of long standing).

ONE MILE

Hampsfell

CARTMEL

B5271 NEWBY BRIDGE
B5277 LEVENS BRIDGE

GRANGE -OVER- SANDS

Grange-over-Sands is blessed with a mild climate, a sheltered and sunny location, fine gardens and lovely woodlands, views across the bay, good shops and an elegant aura of quiet prosperity. It also has Hampsfell.

Hampsfell is a first-rate amenity. It is an elevated ridge of limestone overlooking the Kent Estuary on one side and enjoying a wide prospect of Lakeland on the other. The fell has open access and provides a popular and easy walk with an obvious objective: a stone building known as the Hospice crowning the highest part.

Of Grange's many attractions, Hampsfell is the one most likely to appeal to a semi-retired fellwalker. It is a hill small and unpretentious yet endowed with an air of freedom and space that will recall happy days on greater heights. It is a place for looking northwest, indulging memories, and dreaming.

Limestone pavement
on Hampsfell

Lakeland is almost encircled by a narrow belt of carboniferous limestone. Along the northern boundary of the district it is continuous from a point near St. Bees Head to Shap. In the south it is broken, with considerable intrusions in Furness, around Grange-over-Sands and the Kent Estuary, and on the west side of Kendal.

The Hospice, provided by a pastor of Cartmel in about 1830 for "the shelter and entertainment of travellers over the fell", is a well-built structure of dressed limestone with an outer flight of steps and a flat roof on which is a view-indicator (added later and still in working order in 2010). The open interior offers good shelter and free poetry readings on painted panels on all four walls: these pronounce as follows, doubtful errors and all —

TAKE NOTICE

ALL PERSONS VISITING THIS "HOSPICE" BY PERMISSION OF THE OWNER, ARE REQUESTED TO RESPECT PRIVATE PROPERTY, AND NOT BY ACTS OF WANTON MISCHIEF AND DESTRUCTION SHOW THAT THEY POSSESS MORE MUSCLE THAN BRAIN. I HAVE NO HOPE THAT THIS REQUEST WILL BE ATTENDED TO, FOR AS SOLOMON SAYS "THOUGH THOU SHOULDEST BRAY A FOOL IN A MORTAR AMONG WHEAT WITH A PESTLE, YET WILL NOT HIS FOOLISHNESS DEPART FROM HIM."

G. REMINGTON

O GOD! O GOOD BEYOND COMPARE!
IF THIS THY MEANER WORKS BE FAIR,
IF THUS THY BEAUTY GILD THE SPAN
OF FADED EARTH AND FALLEN MAN,
HOW GLORIOUS MUST THOSE MANSIONS BE
WHERE THY REDEEMED WELL WITH THEE

THE HOSPICE OF HAMPSFELL

THIS HOSPICE AS AN OPEN DOOR,
ALIKE TO WELCOME RICH AND POOR;
A ROOMY SEAT FOR YOUNG AND OLD,
WHERE THEY MAY SCREEN THEM FROM THE COLD:

THREE WINDOWS THAT COMMAND A VIEW,
TO NORTH, TO WEST AND SOUTHWARD TOO,
A FLIGHT OF STEPS REQUIRETH CARE,
THE ROOF WILL SHOW A PROSPECT RARE.

MOUNTAIN & VALE YOU THENCE SURVEY,
THE WINDING STREAMS AND NOBLE BAY;
THE SUN AT NOON THE SHADOW HIDES,
ALONG THE EAST AND WESTERN SIDES:

A LENGTHENED CHAIN HOLDS GUARD AROUND,
TO KEEP THE CATTLE FROM THE GROUND;
KIND READER FREELY TAKE YOUR PLEASURE,
BUT DO NO MISCHIEF TO MY TREASURE:

THE ANSWER

AND IF THE RICH AND POOR SHOULD MEET
I TRUST THEY WILL EACH OTHER GREET,
AND RICH AND POOR AND YOUNG AND OLD
TOGETHER SCREEN THEM FROM THE COLD:

AND AS THE WINDOWS ARE NOT GLASS'D
WE'LL MIND TO LEAVE THE SHUTTERS FAST,
THE "FLIGHT OF STEPS REQUIRETH CARE"
THEN WHY NOT HAVE A HANDRAIL THERE;
THAT FEEBLE OLD AND TIMID FAIR
MAY MOUNT AND VIEW THE PROSPECT RARE.

THE BLUE AND LOFTY MOUNTAIN'S SIDES
THE NOBLE BAY AND STEALTHY TIDES
THAT TREACH'ROUS CREEP ALONG THE SAND
OR LOUDLY DASH UPON THE STRAND.

YON GAILY RIGGED TRIM PLEASURE BOAT
UPON THE GLITTERING WAVES AFLOAT,
THEN (TURNING TO THE WEST) IS SEEN
DEAR CARTMEL'S PEACEFUL VALLEY GREEN;
MID WAVING WOODS AND VERDENT LANDS,
THE FINE OLD CHURCH OF CARTMEL STANDS.

WITHIN WHOSE WALLS IN DAYS OF YORE
HIS PRIESTLY RULE THE PRIOR BORE.
THEN MAY THE LENGTHENING CHAIN AROUND
KEEP ONLY CATTLE FROM THE GROUND;
FOR NO GOOD MAN WOULD THINK IT PLEASURE
TO CLIMB THE FELL TO SPOIL YOUR TREASURE
YOUR OFFER MADE IN KINDLY SPIRIT
I HOPE YOU'LL FIND OUR CONDUCT MERIT;

CARTMEL 1846

Outside, over the doorway, is an inscription that
will be Greek to most visitors.

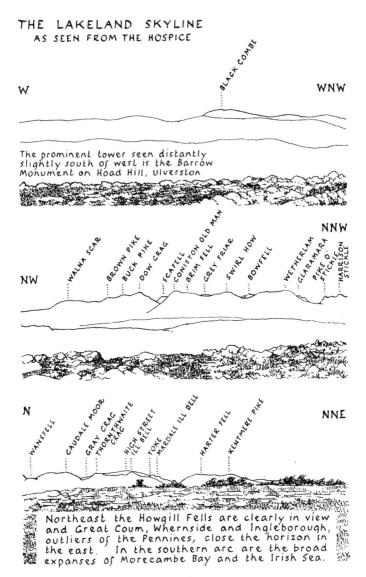

THE LAKELAND SKYLINE
AS SEEN FROM THE HOSPICE

W   BLACK COMBE   WNW

The prominent tower seen distantly
slightly south of west is the Barrow
Monument on Hoad Hill, Ulverston

NW   WALNA SCAR   BROWN PIKE   BUCK PIKE   DOW CRAG   SCAFELL   CONISTON OLD MAN   BRIM FELL   GREY FRIAR   SWIRL HOW   BOWFELL   WETHERLAM   GLARAMARA   PIKE O STICKLE   HARRISON STICKLE   NNW

N   WANSFELL   CAUDALE MOOR   GRAY CRAG   THORNTHWAITE CRAG   HIGH STREET   ILL BELL   YOKE   MARDALE ILL BELL   HARTER FELL   KENTMERE PIKE   NNE

Northeast the Howgill Fells are clearly in view
and Great Coum, Whernside and Ingleborough,
outliers of the Pennines, close the horizon in
the east. In the southern arc are the broad
expanses of Morecambe Bay and the Irish Sea.

56

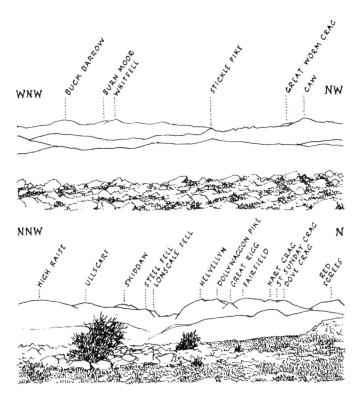

WNW

BUCK BARROW
BURN MOOR
WHITFELL
STICKLE PIKE
GREAT WORM CRAG
CAW

NW

NNW

HIGH RAISE
ULLSCARF
SKIDDAW
STEEL FELL
LONSCALE FELL
HELVELLYN
DOLLYWAGGON PIKE
GREAT RIGG
FAIRFIELD
HART CRAG
St SUNDAY CRAG
DOVE CRAG
RED SCREES

N

Heights and distances:

BLACK COMBE 1969' 17
BUCK BARROW 1799' 17
BURN MOOR 1780' 17½
WHITFELL 1881' 17¼
STICKLE PIKE 1231' 14½
GREAT WORM CRAG 1400' 17
CAW 1735' 14
WALNA SCAR 2035' 13½
BROWN PIKE 2237' 13¾
BUCK PIKE 2441' 14
DOW CRAG 2555' 14¼
SCAFELL 3162' 20½
CONISTON OLD MAN 2635' 14
BRIM FELL 2611' 14½
GREY FRIAR 2536' 15¼

SWIRL HOW 2630' 15½
BOWFELL 2960' 19¼
WETHERLAM 2502' 15¼
GLARAMARA 2569' 21½
PIKE O'STICKLE 2323' 19
HARRISON STICKLE 2415' 18¾
HIGH RAISE 2500' 20
ULLSCARF 2382' 21¼
SKIDDAW 3053' 31¼
STEEL FELL 1811' 20¼
LONSCALE FELL 2344' 30¼
DOLLYWAGGON PIKE 2815' 21
GREAT RIGG 2513' 19¼
FAIRFIELD 2863' 20¼

HART CRAG 2698' 19¾
St SUNDAY CRAG 2756' 21
DOVE CRAG 2598' 19¼
RED SCREES 2546' 18
WANSFELL 1597' 16
CAUDALE MOOR 2502' 19
CRAY CRAG 2286' 20
THORNTHWAITE CRAG 2569' 19
HIGH STREET 2718' 19¼
ILL BELL 2484' 17¾
YOKE 2316' 17
MARDALE ILL BELL 2496' 19¼
HARTER FELL 2552' 19
KENTMERE PIKE 2397' 18

57

WALNA SCAR · WALNA SCAR PASS · BROWN PIKE · BUCK PIKE · DOW CRAG · Goat's HOUSE · CONISTON OLD MAN · BRIM FELL · Levers HAUSE · SWIRL HOW · Swirl HAUSE · BLACK SAILS · WETHERLAM

The beacon on Fell End, looking to the Coniston Fells

From the Clock Tower on Church Hill go past the Post Office and forward up Grange Fell Road, a relentless climb of almost a mile until, opposite the last house, a path on the right, signposted, crosses a short field by stiles and a farm-lane to enter the rough fell at another stile. A path inclining to the right ascends to an area of boulders and scrub and then proceeds smoothly direct to the Hospice (or a detour can be made to the beacon on Fell End).

Return by a path heading northeast from the Hospice, passing a large pile of stones like a tumulus. Paths in this area are vague, but head down to a cart-track alongside Eggerslack Wood, which, followed to the right, leads to a gate at the top of Hampsfell Road with High Farm nearby but not visited. Hampsfell Road winds pleasantly downhill to the town centre, passing a well-preserved limekiln worth looking at.

MAP

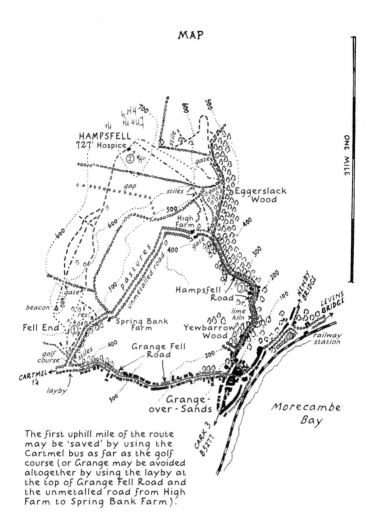

The first uphill mile of the route may be 'saved' by using the Cartmel bus as far as the golf course (or Grange may be avoided altogether by using the layby at the top of Grange Fell Road and the unmetalled road from High Farm to Spring Bank Farm).

Grange has bus services to Barrow in Furness *via* Newby Bridge and Kendal *via* Levens Bridge. Surprisingly in these days of progress, the railway station continues functional, being on the line to West Cumbria and Barrow from Carnforth.

6 Beacon Fell
from Brown Howe

Most walking visitors to Coniston tend to head for the Old Man of Coniston and its surrounding fells, but for families preferring something shorter Beacon Fell makes a splendid introduction to the area.

The walk starts a few miles south of Coniston from the Brown Howe car park beside Coniston Water, and winds pleasantly up a quiet lane before embarking on to Beacon Fell itself, part of the jumble of hills called the Blawith fells. It is only a short rise up to the summit along an easy grassy path, but the panoramic views from here, over the lake and Morecambe Bay as well as the Old Man and its fellow Coniston fells – are better than those from many far higher points in the Lake District. The summit cairn, perched on top of a grassy outcrop, can make children feel like they are on top of the world, even when the height is less than a thousand feet.

Another point of interest on the summit is the logbook that is tucked away in the stones of the cairn for visitors to record their ascents. The book was originally left in the cairn in a wooden box, though it has been replaced more recently by a blue tin, which has also housed climbers' notes and other mementoes like champagne corks. It is maintained by locals and fans of the fell, and you can read some of the entertaining comments of the last few years at www.beaconfell.blogspot. com. The book and its tin occasionally go missing or have to be replaced when full up, but if you find it in the cairn, add your own details and tuck it safely back in for others to enjoy.

The round trip to Beacon Fell should take no more than a couple of hours, but a startlingly varied amount of terrain and scenery are packed into such a short walk. The lower slopes of the climb mix grass, juniper and bracken, while higher up there is abundant heather and rocky outcrops. The colours are bold and spectacular most of the year round, though autumn, when the hues are rich and golden, is a particularly good time to visit. The fell even has a tarn of its own, not far from the summit on the way back to Brown Howe. Beacon Tarn is a large and delightful pool in which walkers and dogs have been known to enjoy swimming, and as water in the Lake District goes, it is not too cold – though nor is it what most people would consider warm, and care is obviously required if you want to have a dip.

As an introduction to fellwalking, Beacon Fell is hard to beat, providing examples of many of the things that make the Lake District unique and special. 'Beacon Fell ranks amongst the most delectable of the lesser heights of Lakeland,' notes Wainwright. 'It is an epitome of all that appeals to fellwalkers.'

From *The Outlying Fells of Lakeland*

Distance 3½ miles (5.6km)

Ascent 800 feet (245m)

Start and finish point The pay-and-display Brown Howe car park on the shores of Coniston Water (SD 290 911). You may be able to park for free on one of two lay-bys a little further back towards Ulverston on the A5084, though these can fill up quickly in the summer

Ordnance Survey maps Explorer OL6; Landranger 96

Getting there
The Brown Howe car park is just off the A5084 from Torver to Ulverston. It is about 2 miles (3.2km) south of Torver on the left-hand side if coming from that direction.

The starting point is served by the X12 bus, which stops near by on its route between Ulverston and Coniston, stopping at villages including Greenodd, Spark Bridge, Lowick Bridge, Blawith and Torver in between. There are only about six services daily in either direction, and no service at all on Sundays, so plan your itinerary carefully. The most convenient train station is Ulverston, which connects to the starting point in just under half an hour on the X12 bus.

Facilities, food and drink
The Brown Howe car park has public toilets with baby changing facilities, and a nice picnic spot by the lake. You can launch boats from here and paddle or swim on warmer days.

The nearest pubs are 2 miles (3.2km) away in Torver. The characterful, fifteenth-century Church House Inn (015394 41282, www.churchhouseinntorver.com) and the more modern Wilson Arms (015394 41237, www.thewilsonarms. co.uk) both offer good food and rooms to stay.

More pubs and the nearest shops are 2½ miles (4km) north of Torver in Coniston. The Black Bull, home of the Coniston Brewery (015394 41335, www.blackbullconiston. co.uk), and the Ship Inn (015394 41224, www.shipinn.info) are particularly recommended. Coniston also has attractions including the Ruskin Museum, which has interesting material relating to Donald Campbell's speed record attempts on the lake as well as displays about John Ruskin (015394 41164, www.ruskinmuseum.com); and Ruskin's home at Brantwood, which has wonderful gardens as well as interesting tours of the house and a very child-friendly café with a box of toys and books (015395 41396, www.brantwood.org.uk). Trips out on Coniston Water are also popular, either on the lake cruises run by Coniston Launch (017687 75753, www.conistonlaunch. co.uk; year-round service), or on the magnificent Victorian steam yacht *Gondola*, run by the National Trust (015394 32733, www.nationaltrust.org.uk/gondola; April to October only). Both services run from Coniston Pier – which also offers the excellent Bluebird Café by the water (015394 41649, www. thebluebirdcafe.com) – and stop at Brantwood for anyone who wants to combine a visit. There is a children's playground close to the pier on Lake Road.

Directions

1 Return to the main road from the car park. Cross it carefully and turn left. After about 110 yards (100m), turn right on to a narrow road. Follow this up for nearly ¾ mile (1.2km), and where it turns on a hairpin bend to the right, leave it to the left on a clear grassy path that leads towards electricity cables overhead. Just before the cables, bend slightly left at a fork of paths to go underneath them, then climb up ahead through the bracken up to a ridge, after which Beacon Fell can be seen up ahead.

2 Keep climbing steadily along this grassy path, crossing two small streams. Further up, there is a short scramble over rock and slate, but this is easy and soon gives way to grass again. The summit cairn (SD 278 907) is a few steps to the left of the path, hidden by some low crags. See Wainwright's notes for details of the fells on the skyline; the tarn you can see to the left of Coniston Water is a disused reservoir.

3 Continue on from the summit, descending slightly to a col. Here, ignore the side path to the left, and continue ahead over the promontory, after which Beacon Tarn comes into view below. Descend towards the tarn, bending right at a large rock covered in heather to drop down to the water's edge at its head (SD 275 903).

4 Walk away from the head of the tarn to pick up a grassy path, heading north to a col between two heights. The path continues on to the right of a large marshy hollow in the hills, then descends and traverses the west side of Beacon Fell. This is now the Cumbria Way, the long-distance route that links Ulverston and Carlisle via some of the Lake District's best scenery. Further on, ignore a side path to the left, before dropping down to the electricity cables and the hairpin bend in the road left earlier. Turn right along the road back to the A5084, then left for the car park.

Beacon Fell
836'

800 feet of ascent

from BROWN HOWE

3½ miles
2 hours

On Ordnance maps the summit is marked 'Beacon' (part of Blawith Fells)

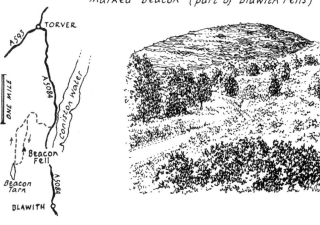

Beacon Fell ranks amongst the most delectable of the lesser heights of Lakeland. It is an epitome of all that appeals to fellwalkers. The approach is a joy: lovely and colourful terrain rich in trees and dense thickets of juniper relieved occasionally by marshy flats of myrtle and dry banks of bracken. Higher, grey rocks outcrop in haphazard array and heather and bilberry carpet the rough ground. The paths are enchanting, full of little surprises, while the streams are crystal clear. There is a tarn, too, hidden in a fold of the hills. But it is the summit, abrupt and rocky, and the far-reaching view that make the ascent so worth while. One can recline in comfort here and almost feel sorry for youngsters who, at this moment, are toiling up Great Gable.

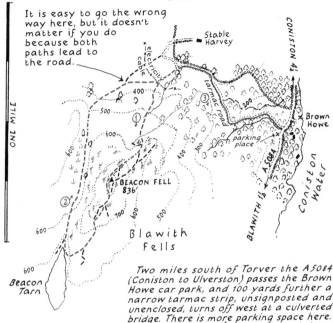

It is easy to go the wrong way here, but it doesn't matter if you do because both paths lead to the road.

Stable Harvey

CONISTON 4½

electricity cable

400

500

600

600

Brown Howe

BLAWITH 1½   A5084

Coniston Water

parking place

tarmac road

① ② ③

BEACON FELL 836'

Beacon Tarn

700   600   500

Blawith Fells

ONE MILE

Two miles south of Torver the A5084 (Coniston to Ulverston) passes the Brown Howe car park, and 100 yards further a narrow tarmac strip, unsignposted and unenclosed, turns off west at a culverted bridge. There is more parking space here. Cars may be taken along this byroad for ¼ of a mile and there parked, but walking on it is so enjoyable, fringed by a tangle of bog myrtle, juniper, bracken and woodland trees, that it is a pity to hurry over it on wheels. At the upper parking place, on a hairpin bend, a wide green path leads away to the left. Follow this, but just before reaching an overhead cable take a thin track branching up left through the bracken, leading to a charming route along an indefinite ridge amongst low outcrops. Two streams are crossed, the second in wet ground. When the path veers off to the left aim for and climb a rocky gully (easy, even for us) so reaching the summit cairn, which is defended by low crags: a delightful spot. Hidden in the cairn is a blue box containing a visitors' book. Continue south along the top, ignoring a path on the left and bearing left to a little promontory where Beacon Tarn comes into view. Descend right to rejoin the main path and go down to the head of the tarn by turning right at a prominent rock draped with bell heather. Join a path from the tarn going north over a low col and skirting a marshy hollow (bog myrtle rampant) and a pond (bogbean rampant in summer), then descending through bracken and bearing right to rejoin the outward path at the cable and repeat the walk on tarmac to the A5084.

THE VIEW

The view is restricted by the nearby Coniston Fells, which conceal central Lakeland, but in other directions, especially northeast, is uninterrupted by intermediate heights. The full length of Coniston Water is seen, but of greater interest is the panorama to the south, where Morecambe Bay and the Crake and Duddon estuaries make great indentations of the coastline of the Irish Sea. Industrial smoke rises from the Furness peninsula and the huge quarries of Kirkby Moor appear on the skyline to the right of a wind farm. Far away to the east are the Pennines.

The rocky gully

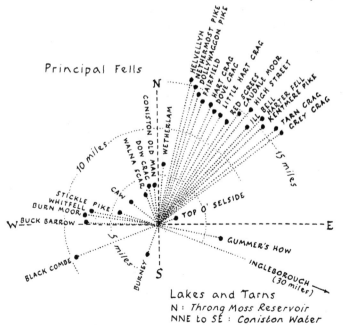

Principal Fells

N

HELVELLYN
DOLLYWAGGON PIKE
DOETHERMOST PIKE
FAIRFIELD
HART CRAG
DOVE CRAG
LITTLE HART CRAG
RED SCREES
CAUDALE MOOR
HIGH STREET
ILL BELL
HARTER FELL
KENTMERE PIKE
TARN CRAG
GREY CRAG

CONISTON OLD MAN
WETHERLAM
DOW CRAG
WALNA SCAR

10 miles

15 miles

STICKLE PIKE
WHITFELL
BURN MOOR
CAW

TOP O' SELSIDE

W — BUCK BARROW — E

5 miles

GUMMER'S HOW

BLACK COMBE

BURNEY

INGLEBOROUGH
(30 miles)

S

Lakes and Tarns
N : *Throng Moss Reservoir*
NNE to SE : *Coniston Water*

66

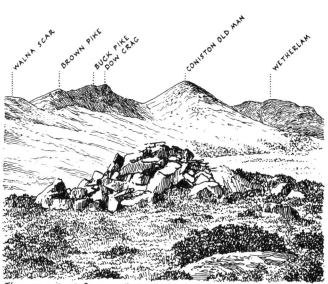

WALNA SCAR   BROWN PIKE   BUCK PIKE DOW CRAG   CONISTON OLD MAN   WETHERLAM

The summit of Beacon Fell, looking north to the Coniston Fells

Beacon Tarn

7 Helm Crag
from Grasmere

'The virtues of Helm Crag have not been lauded enough,' writes Wainwright in his *Pictorial Guide to the Central Fells*. 'It gives an exhilarating little climb, a brief essay in real mountaineering, and in a region where all is beautiful, it makes a notable contribution to the natural charms and attractions of Grasmere.'

If he were around today, Wainwright would almost certainly consider that Helm Crag's virtues have been lauded quite enough, since it is now one of the most popular walks from one of the most popular villages in the Lake District. But despite the crowds on summer days it is well worth the effort, and remains a classic walk from this pretty Lakeland village. As Wainwright suggests, it offers an excellent introduction to fellwalking and an example of the grand fells in miniature – the views from the top are so good that it is easy to forget that the peak is barely 1,300 feet (400m) high.

It is a perfect walk for families too, most of whom should be able to get up and down within a morning or afternoon, though on a nice day it is easy to spend much more time enjoying the views. Partly because they are now so well trodden, the paths up to the top are easy, both underfoot and to follow, and children will enjoy the spectacular rocky summit area, though care is needed as there are some steep drops around. This is one of the few fells for which going up and down by the same way is recommended; even Wainwright, who favoured a circular route over a straight there-and-back wherever possible, conceded that the route up via Easedale Road and Goody Bridge is the best way both up and down.

Helm Crag is one of the most distinctive fells in the Lake District, and one of its most widely recognised, even by people who have never been near it. Perhaps because of the affection in which it is held, it is probably the one with the most nicknames too, mostly drawn from the shape of the summit's rocks from various directions; the most popular is 'The Lion and the Lamb', and others include 'The Old Lady Playing the Organ' and 'The Howitzer'.

The last nickname especially gives some idea of the rocky peak of Helm Crag, which rises sharply up from the summit area. It is one of only a few summits in the Lake District that require a certain degree of rock climbing skill to reach, and a scramble up to perch on the top is not recommended for small children, though older ones may fancy the challenge. Just before the rocks there is a grassy plateau on which to rest. If you do decide that discretion is the better part of valour, you will be in very good company indeed – as Wainwright admits in his notes, despite plenty of ascents up one of his favourite fells, the true peak remained beyond his daring.

From *Book Three: The Central Fells*

Distance 3 miles (4.8km)

Ascent 1,100 feet (335m)

Start and finish point The pay-and-display Broadgate Meadow car park in Grasmere (NY 338 077)

Ordnance Survey maps Explorer OL7; Landranger 90

Getting there

The Broadgate Meadow car park is on the northern edge of Grasmere, off the B5287 that runs through the town. The B5287 connects up at either end of the village with the A591.

Grasmere is well served by buses. The 555 stops in the centre of the village, close to the start of the walk, on its way between Lancaster and Keswick, and runs every hour in each direction (every two hours on Sundays and public holidays). Stops in between include Kendal, Staveley, Windermere, Troutbeck Bridge, Ambleside and Rydal. From late March to late October, the 599 bus – The Lakeland Experience – runs every 20 minutes between Bowness and Grasmere, stopping at Windermere and Ambleside as well as popular tourist spots like the Lake District National Park Visitor Centre and Rydal Mount on the way.

Anyone making for Grasmere by train should head for Windermere station, from which both the 555 and 599 buses pick up.

Facilities, food and drink

You don't have to walk far in Grasmere to find food and drink. Particularly recommended is the family-friendly Jumble Room restaurant on Langdale Road (015394 35188, www.thejumbleroom.co.uk), which has toys and books for children as well as very good organic food. Pub-wise, Tweedies bar at the Dale Lodge Hotel on Red Bank Road (015394 35300, www.tweediesbargrasmere.co.uk) has open fires and good food and beers. The Miller Howe Café, close to the start and finish of this walk on Broadgate (015394 35234), is among several options for tea and cakes, while Lancrigg, off the top of Easedale Road on your left as you return from Helm Crag, is a renowned vegetarian restaurant that also serves afternoon teas and the like (015394 35317, www.lancrigg.co.uk).

There is plenty more to do in Grasmere before or after a climb up Helm Crag. Most visitors fit in a hour or two at William Wordsworth's old home at Dove Cottage (015394 35544, www.wordsworth.org.uk), which has interesting displays and family activities in school holidays as well as tours of the house. No visit to Grasmere would be complete without picking up treats at the Grasmere Gingerbread Shop at the corner of the churchyard of St Oswald's Church (015394 35428, www.grasmeregingerbread.co.uk); it makes an excellent alternative to Kendal Mint Cake for an energy boost on the fells. Beside the shop is a limited information centre, housed by the National Trust (015394 35655), though the nearest main centre is in Ambleside (0844 225 0544, www.thehubofambleside.co.uk). The car park has a children's playground near by, plus seats overlooking the Rothay river for picnics.

Directions

1 Leave the car park to rejoin the main road through the village by Grasmere Hall. Cross the road carefully, turn left, and walk towards the village. Opposite the Sam Read bookshop – one of the best bookshops in Cumbria – turn right up Easedale Road. This quiet road passes a youth hostel, Quaker meeting house and guest house; soon after this, pass through a small gate on the left hand side of the road and take the footpath parallel to the road. The path rejoins the road at Goody Bridge (NY 333 081).

2 Cross and continue ahead up the road, ignoring the turn to the right. It soon narrows into a one-track lane serving a cluster of houses. After passing Bouthwaite Barn, at a junction of paths bend right, signposted for Far Easedale and Helm Crag. The rocky path climbs, passes through a wide wooden gate, and reaches another junction 55 yards (50m) later. Bend right here, the way again signposted for Helm Crag, and soon turn right at a T-junction of paths, the way indicated by a cairn.

3 The path now starts to get steep as it zig zags up the fellside, but the way up is very clear, at first over slab steps and later grassy slopes. Take care with children throughout – the stone can be slippery, and the drops off to the side are steep in places. On the summit area you will find several points that look like tops, but the path takes you up to the highest one (NY 327 093). The true peak of Helm Crag is an outcrop of jagged rocks; see the introduction to this walk and decide whether or not you want to tackle it.

4 Descend by the same route, enjoying the views you had your back to earlier, and take particular care in the wet. When you reach Goody Bridge, you can take an alternative way back to Grasmere by following the footpath parallel to the road beyond the point at which you joined it earlier. The way is indicated by green National Trust arrows, and eventually joins another road. Turn left back into Grasmere, then left again for the car park.

Helm Crag

1329'

affectionately known as
'The Lion and The Lamb'

HELM ▲
CRAG

Grasmere●

MILES
0   1   2

This is the smallest (and most accurate!) map in the book

from Grasmere

NATURAL FEATURES

Helm Crag may well be the best-known of all Lakeland fells, and possibly even the best-known hill in the country. Generations of waggonette and motor-coach tourists have been tutored to recognise its appearance in the Grasmere landscape: it is the one feature of their Lakeland tour they hail at sight, and in unison, but the cry on their lips is not "Helm Crag!" but "The Lion and the Lamb!" — in a variety of dialects. The resemblance of the summit rocks to a lion is so striking that recognition, from several viewpoints, is instant; yet, oddly, the outline most like Leo is not the official 'Lion' at all: in fact there are two lions, each with a lamb, and each guards one end of the summit ridge as though set there by architectural design. The summit is altogether a rather weird and fantastic place, well worth not merely a visit but a detailed and leisurely exploration. Indeed the whole fell, although of small extent, is unusually interesting; its very appearance is challenging; its sides are steep, rough and craggy; its top bristles; it *looks* irascible, like a shaggy terrier in a company of sleek foxhounds, for all around are loftier and smoother fells, circling the pleasant vale of Grasmere out of which Helm Crag rises so abruptly.

The fell is not isolated, nor independent of others, for it is the termination of a long ridge enclosing Far Easedale in a graceful curve on north and east and rising, finally, to the rocky peak of Calf Crag. It drains quickly, is dry underfoot, and has no streams worthy of mention.

The virtues of Helm Crag have not been lauded enough. It gives an exhilarating little climb, a brief essay in real mountaineering, and, in a region where all is beautiful, it makes a notable contribution to the natural charms and attractions of Grasmere.

outline of
STEEL FELL

DUNMAIL
RAISE
↓

THE
GREENBURN
VALLEY

*summit
scene*

73

MAP

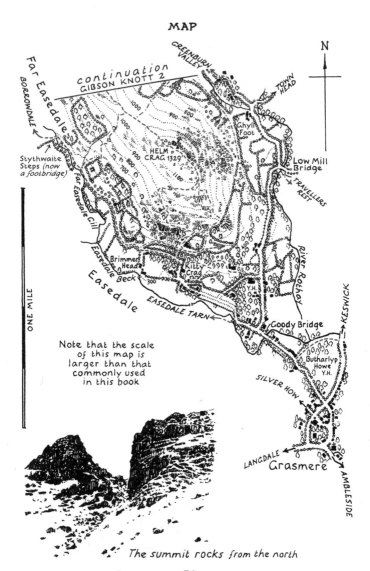

N

continuation
GIBSON KNOTT 2

Far Easedale

BORROWDALE

GREENBURN VALLEY

TOWN HEAD

Ghyll Foot

1000

1000

900

800

HELM CRAG 1329

900

1100

1100

Low Mill Bridge

TRAVELLERS REST

Stythwaite Steps (now a footbridge)

Far Easedale Gill

700

Easedale Gill

800

River Rothay

Brimmer Head

Kitty Crag

Easedale Beck

Easedale

300

Y.H.

EASEDALE TARN

Goody Bridge

KESWICK

Note that the scale of this map is larger than that commonly used in this book

Butharlyp Howe Y.H.

SILVER HOW

ONE MILE

LANGDALE

Grasmere

AMBLESIDE

The summit rocks from the north

ASCENT FROM GRASMERE
1100 feet of ascent : 1½ miles

This is one of the few hills where ascent and descent by the same route is recommended, the new path depicted here being much the best way both up and down. An alternative route (shown on the map but not on this diagram) has nothing in its favour.

If, however, Helm Crag is to be a part only of the day's programme (e.g. the circuit of Far Easedale or the Greenburn valley) it is better reserved for descent, for then the Vale of Grasmere will be directly in view ahead; and this fair scene is at its best when the shadows of evening are lengthening, with the Langdales silhouetted in rugged outline against the sunset. Tarry long over this exquisite picture of serenity and peace, and memorise it for the long winter of exile!

looking north-west

This is a splendid little climb ; if it has a fault it is that it is too short. But for the evening of the day of arrival in Grasmere on a walking holiday it is just the thing : an epitome of Lakeland concentrated in the space of two hours — and an excellent foretaste of happy days to come.

THE SUMMIT

Rocks at the north-west end of the summit ridge, *known by various names:*
(a) The 'Lion Couchant, *or, more popularly,* The Lion and The Lamb. *(as seen from the road below Dunmail Raise)*
(b) The Howitzer *(as seen from Dunmail Raise)*

The highest point of the rocks is the true summit of the fell

   In scenic values, the summits of many high mountains are a disappointment after the long toil of ascent, yet here, on the top of little Helm Crag, a midget of a mountain, is a remarkable array of rocks, upstanding and fallen, of singular interest and fascinating appearance, that yield a quality of reward out of all proportion to the short and simple climb. The uppermost inches of Scafell and Helvellyn and Skiddaw can show nothing like Helm Crag's crown of shattered and petrified stone : indeed, its highest point, a pinnacle of rock airily thrust out above a dark abyss, is not to be attained by walking and is brought underfoot only by precarious manoeuvres of the body. This is one of the very few summits in Lakeland reached only by climbing rocks, and it is certainly (but not for that reason alone) one of the very best.
continued

THE SUMMIT

continued

The summit ridge is 250 yards in length and is adorned at each end by fangs of rock overtopping the fairly level path. Between these towers there have been others in ages past but all that remains of them now is a chaos of collapsed boulders, choking a strange depression that extends the full length of the summit on the north-east side. The depression is bounded by a secondary ridge, and this in turn descends craggily to an even more strange depression, in appearance resembling a huge ditch cleft straight as a furrow across the breast of the fell for 300 yards ; or, more romantically, a deep moat defending the turreted wall of the castle above. This surprising feature, which will not be seen unless searched for, will doubtless be readily explained by geologists (or antiquaries ?) ; to the unlearned beholder it seems likely to be the result of some ancient natural convulsion that caused the side of the fell to slip downwards a few yards before coming to rest. This ditch is also bounded on its far side by a parallel ridge or parapet (narrow, and an interesting walk) beyond which the fellside plunges down almost precipitously to the valley, falling in juniper-clad crags.

Care is necessary when exploring the boulder-strewn depressions on the summit, especially if the rocks are greasy. There are many good natural shelters here, and some dangerous clefts and fissures and holes, so well protected from the weather that summer flowers are to be found in bloom in their recesses as late as mid-winter.

The south-west side of the summit ridge consists mainly of bracken slopes and are of little interest in their upper reaches.

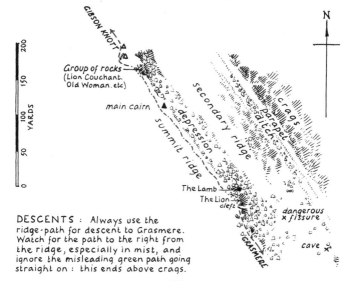

DESCENTS : Always use the ridge-path for descent to Grasmere. Watch for the path to the right from the ridge, especially in mist, and ignore the misleading green path going straight on : this ends above crags.

THE SUMMIT

Rocks at the north-west end of the summit-ridge known as The Old Woman Playing the Organ *from their appearance when seen from Tongue Gill and the vicinity of Easedale Tarn*

Rocks at the south-east end of the summit-ridge. *These form the* OFFICIAL Lion and The Lamb *(as seen from the Swan Hotel, Grasmere). The lion's head is the O.S. 'station' (altitude 1306') but is not quite the highest point of the fell*

THE VIEW

This is the view from the cairn on the summit ridge — whether it coincides with the view from the highest point the author will never know for his several attempts to mount to the rocky pate of the Lion Couchant have all been defeated by a lack of resolution; but probably it is the same. In any case, most visitors will be content to study the prospect from the comparative security of the cairn on the ridge.

continued

continued
The Vale of Grasmere is best displayed from the head of the other (official) Lion, which even the author found a simple ascent, (although deeply conscious of precipices all around).

Principal Fells

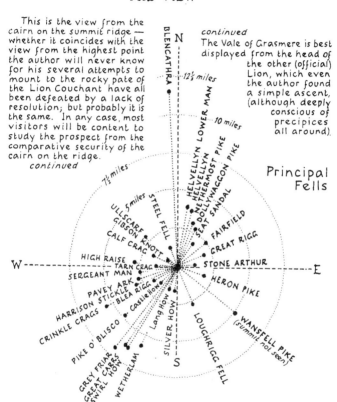

The prominent height south-south-east (to the right of Loughrigg Fell) is Gummer's How, 13 miles distant at the foot of Windermere.

Lakes and Tarns

SE: *Windermere (upper reach)*
SSE: *Grasmere*
SSE: *Esthwaite Water*
WSW: *Easedale Tarn*

This corner was reserved for an announcement that the author had succeeded in surmounting the highest point, but no such announcement was made.

Tarn Crag
across Far Easedale
from the slopes of Helm Crag

The north-east face
from Low Mill Bridge

RIDGE ROUTE

To GIBSON KNOTT, 1379'
1 mile : NW, then W
Depression at 1050'
400 feet of ascent
An interesting ridge climb

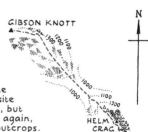

Two big cairns indicate the way off Helm Crag. A narrow path crosses the depression and continues up the opposite slope; it does not keep to the ridge, but crosses it from left to right and back again, winding charmingly between rock outcrops. The cairned summit rises across a shallow hollow.

ONE MILE

Helm Crag, from the path to Gibson Knott

8 Silver How
from Grasmere

Along with Helm Crag, Silver How is one of the best-loved fell walks from Grasmere. Each makes for a fine morning or afternoon excursion from the popular village and achieves a virtually identical distance and height, and no excuses are needed for including both options.

Silver How is a less distinctive fell than its instantly recognisable counterpart to the north, and as Wainwright notes its summit is not so spectacular. In fact, in common with several other now-popular fells, it might have remained simply one of a cluster of tops along the ridge in the area had he not singled out its merits in his *Pictorial Guides*. But it is a fine place to rest and enjoy the outstanding views over the Grasmere village and valley, several lakes and tarns, and fells including the Helvellyn range and the Langdale Pikes. 'This is probably as good a place as any for a newcomer to the district to appreciate its variety and unique charm,' says Wainwright.

The routes up and down Silver How that are described here are excellent too, providing a tour of the rough slopes that Wainwright describes in his introduction, and which take in juniper, bracken and the crags and stone that, when viewed in the right light, give the fell its name. The return leg also passes Wray Gill, a fine example of the streams that tumble down from the fells and keep the lakes and tarns stocked.

The paths here also show signs of the work of Fix the Fells, a project to repair footpaths across the Lake District that suffer erosion and other damage. The initiative is viewed by many fellwalkers as something of a mixed blessing – given the pounding the paths now get, the work is undoubtedly needed and it will help to preserve them for years to come, but the tidying up inevitably impacts on the pristine landscape, taming the fells into places less wild than some would like. On the whole the footpath work is sympathetically done, and families are more often than not grateful for the improved access it gives to the fells for children who find the rougher fellsides hard going. Even after the hard work of the volunteers who support Fix the Fells, the walk up and down Silver How remains steep in places and a scramble at the top, so it may be unsuitable for very small children.

From *Book Three: The Central Fells*

Distance 3 miles (4.8km)

Ascent 1,100 feet (335m)

Start and finish point The Red Bank Road pay-and-display car park, near the nursery at the southern end of the village on the road between Grasmere and Langdale (NY 335 074)

Ordnance Survey maps Explorer OL7; Landranger 90

Getting there

Take the A591 to Grasmere from either north or south, then pick up the B5287 that runs through the village itself. Look for the signs to the Langdale valley and the large garden centre that is adjacent to the car park. Make sure you don't park in the nursery, as staff there are strict on enforcing customer parking.

To avoid the high car parking fees and enjoy the views on the way, take a bus into Grasmere. The 555 runs between Lancaster and Kendal in the south and Keswick in the north every hour (every two hours on Sundays and public holidays). Between late March and late October, the 599 or Lakeland Experience bus runs every 20 minutes between Bowness and Grasmere, stopping at Windermere, Ambleside and Rydal on the way. You can take either of these buses from Windermere station if arriving in the area by train.

Facilities, food and drink

The centre of Grasmere, a short walk from the car park, has plenty of cafés and shops from which you can make up a picnic for this walk. Baldry's Café on Red Lion Square is particularly friendly and serves good cake for tired walkers (015934 35301). The Miller Howe Café, right by the finish of the walk on Broadgate, is also good for afternoon tea (015394 35234).

Other family-friendly eating options in the village include the Jumble Room restaurant on Langdale Road (015394 35188, www.thejumbleroom.co.uk), while The Rowan Tree on Stock Lane has a nice riverside terrace (015394 35528). Good pubs include Tweedies bar at the Dale Lodge Hotel on Red Bank Road (015394 35300, www.tweediesbargrasmere. co.uk) and, a short way out of the village to the north, the Traveller's Rest, a characterful sixteenth-century coaching inn (015394 35604, www.lakedistrictinns.co.uk). Most of the many hotels, including the Gold Rill on Red Bank Road near the car park for the walk (015394 35486, www.goldrill. co.uk), serve food to non-residents.

Many of the most popular visitor attractions in Grasmere are associated with its most famous resident, William Wordsworth. His old house at Dove Cottage (015394 35544, www.wordsworth.org.uk) has tours, displays and things for children in school holidays, while St Oswald's Church has his grave. Close by the churchyard is the famous Grasmere Gingerbread Shop, usually with queues and wonderful smells coming out of the door (015394 35428, www.grasmeregingerbread.co.uk). A third stop on the Wordsworth tour is another of his homes, Rydal Mount, a short drive away in Rydal, which has house tours, gardens and a tearoom (015394 33002, www.rydalmount.co.uk). For more about what to do in and around Grasmere, call in at the tourist information centre in Ambleside (0844 225 0544, www.thehubofambleside.co.uk).

Directions

1 Turn left on to the Langdale road, soon passing the Gold Rill hotel. The quiet road passes over a stream. A few steps on, in front of the drive up to Kelbarrow, leave it on a path to the right, indicated by a public footpath sign. The path goes through a wooden gate, then climbs with dry stone walls on either side to another one. Silver How is now directly ahead, and the way is very clear, first crossing a grassy slope to pass through another gate, and then climbing with a wall to your left by a stream. Cross the stream and keep climbing, still with the wall close by on your left.

2 At the point where the path and wall start to descend, marked by a pile of stones (NY 327 064), leave it on another path to the right. It climbs up the fellside, and further up passes through a scree gully, though stone steps make most of it easy going. Soon after the steps run out, by another cairn, take the path to the left. This is more of a scramble for a while, but it soon returns to grassier slopes and winds round to the summit of Silver How (NY 325 066); the path is indistinct in places, and is part of something of a maze of ways to the top, but the highest point to aim for should be obvious. There are plenty of rocks to perch on and grassy spots to spread a picnic out on here, and the views down towards Grasmere lake are superb.

3 With the lake to your back, drop off the summit in a northerly direction and pick up a clear path downhill. It is marked by intermittent cairns and after a while drops more steeply to cross a stream, Wray Gill (NY 324 072). The stream can be heavy after rain, though it is crossable with care. The path continues to wind down to grassier slopes, crossed by a network of dry stone walls, then leads you down between two walls to emerge at a couple of white buildings. Turn right on to the narrow road, which weaves pleasantly down into Grasmere. You emerge with the Miller Howe Café on your left; take the first road on your right for the car park, or continue on for a stroll around Grasmere.

Silver How

1292'

Grasmere ●
SILVER HOW ▲
Chapel ●
Stile
Elterwater ●

LOUGHRIGG
▲ FELL

MILES
0 1 2 3 4

from Loughrigg Terrace

NATURAL FEATURES

A lovely name for a lovely fell : Silver How is delightful. Not because the summit is remarkable, except for the view; the grassy top is, indeed, the least of its attractions. It is the rough slopes that delight the eye, especially on the Grasmere side, for the intermingling of crag and conifer, juniper and bracken, is landscape artistry at its best. A wealth of timber adorns the lower slopes and trees persist into the zone of crags fringing the summit. Fine waterfalls are another characteristic, though none is well known: Blindtarn Gill, Wray Gill, and Megs Gill, the latter the best, all have spectacular cataracts.

Silver How is a prominent height on the wide and broken ridge that may be said to start with Loughrigg Fell and continue, dividing Langdale and Easedale, to High Raise, the highest point.

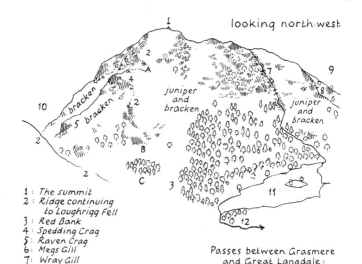

looking north-west

1 : The summit
2 : Ridge continuing
    to Loughrigg Fell
3 : Red Bank
4 : Spedding Crag
5 : Raven Crag
6 : Megs Gill
7 : Wray Gill
8 : Blindtarn Gill
9 : Easedale   10 : Great Langdale
11 : Grasmere   12 : River Rothay

Passes between Grasmere
and Great Langdale :
A : via Megs Gill
B : via Hunting Stile
C : via Red Bank

MAP

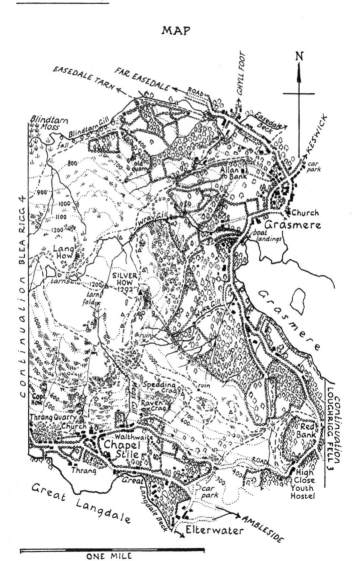

ONE MILE

88

ASCENT FROM GRASMERE
1100 feet of ascent : 1½ miles

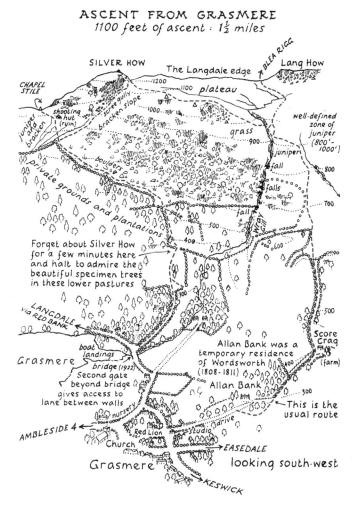

SILVER HOW

The Langdale edge

BLEA RIGG

Lang How

CHAPEL STILE

1200

1100 plateau

shooting hut (ruin)

scree gully

juniper and bracken

bracken slope

1000

grass

900

well-defined zone of juniper (800'-1000')

juniper

boulders

fall

falls

800

700

private grounds and plantations

scree

fall

500

WAY

400

600

Forget about Silver How for a few minutes here and halt to admire the beautiful specimen trees in these lower pastures

300

LANGDALE via RED BANK

500

Score Crag (farm)

boat landings

bridge (1922)

Grasmere

Second gate beyond bridge gives access to lane between walls

Allan Bank was a temporary residence of Wordsworth (1808-1811)

400

Allan Bank

300

This is the usual route

nursery

drive

AMBLESIDE 4

Red Lion

studio

Church

EASEDALE

Grasmere

looking south-west

KESWICK

Two routes are given, both supremely beautiful walks. The views are charming. Alternatively, the summit may be reached from any of the ridge-passes to Langdale.

89

ASCENT FROM ELTERWATER
1200 feet of ascent : 2¼ miles

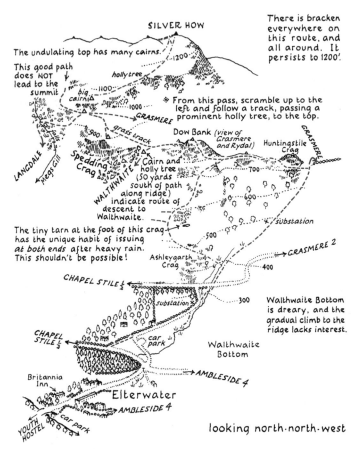

SILVER HOW

The undulating top has many cairns.

There is bracken everywhere on this route, and all around. It persists to 1200'.

This good path does NOT lead to the summit

1200

holly tree

1100

big cairn

1000

GRASMERE

✻ From this pass, scramble up to the left and follow a track, passing a prominent holly tree, to the top.

900

grass track

Dow Bank (view of Grasmere and Rydal)

Huntingstile Crag

GRASMERE

Spedding Crag

LANGDALE

Megs Gill

WALTHWAITE

Cairn and holly tree (50 yards south of path along ridge) indicate route of descent to Walthwaite.

700

600

substation

The tiny tarn at the foot of this crag has the unique habit of issuing at both ends after heavy rain. This shouldn't be possible!

500

Ashleygarth Crag

GRASMERE 2

400

CHAPEL STILE ¾

substation

300

Walthwaite Bottom is dreary, and the gradual climb to the ridge lacks interest.

CHAPEL STILE ½

car park

Walthwaite Bottom

Britannia Inn

AMBLESIDE 4

Elterwater

AMBLESIDE 4

YOUTH HOSTEL

car park

looking north·north·west

After a dull start, interest quickens when the ridge is reached (at either of the points indicated) and the view opens out over Grasmere; thereafter the walk increases in beauty. Winter colourings are very good.

ASCENT FROM CHAPEL STILE
1050 feet of ascent : 1¼ miles

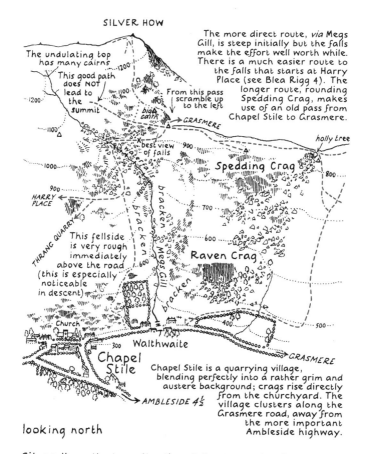

SILVER HOW

The undulating top
has many cairns

This good path
does NOT
lead to
the
summit

1200

1100

1200

1100

From this pass
scramble up
to the left

big cairn

→ GRASMERE

The more direct route, *via Megs
Gill*, is steep initially but the falls
make the effort well worth while.
There is a much easier route to
the falls that starts at Harry
Place (see Blea Rigg 4). The
longer route, rounding
Spedding Crag, makes
use of an old pass from
Chapel Stile to Grasmere.

holly tree

best view
of falls

900

Spedding Crag

800

1000

Megs Gill falls

800

bracken

700

HARRY
PLACE

900

600

THRANG QUARRY

This fellside
is very rough
immediately
above the road
(this is especially
noticeable
in descent)

bracken

Megs Gill

Raven Crag

600

bracken

500

400

Church

Walthwaite

GRASMERE

300

Chapel
Stile

Chapel Stile is a quarrying village,
blending perfectly into a rather grim and
austere background; crags rise directly
from the churchyard. The
village clusters along the
Grasmere road, away from
the more important
Ambleside highway.

→ AMBLESIDE 4½

looking north

Silver How displays its finest features to Grasmere
and turns a comparatively dowdy back to Langdale;
nevertheless the short climb is attractive and the
views when the ridge is reached are very charming.

THE SUMMIT

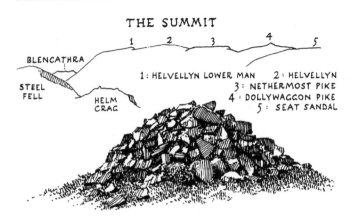

BLENCATHRA

STEEL FELL

HELM CRAG

1: HELVELLYN LOWER MAN   2: HELVELLYN
3: NETHERMOST PIKE
4: DOLLYWAGGON PIKE
5: SEAT SANDAL

The top of the fell is extensive and forms several rounded elevations, most of them cairned, but the actual summit is conspicuously situated above the steep Grasmere face. The paths across the top are little better than narrow sheep-tracks in the grass.

DESCENTS: Commence all descents from the small depression 100 yards west-south-west, turning right for Grasmere and left for Langdale via Megs Gill. Do not attempt descents *directly* to Grasmere: a wall of crags lies below the summit on this side. *In mist* the paths will not be easy to follow; if they are lost in the early stages keep on in the same direction and they will re-appear.

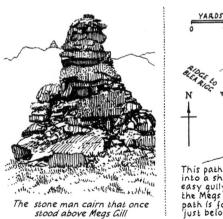

The stone man cairn that once stood above Megs Gill

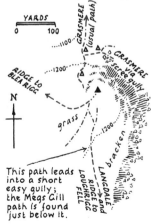

This path leads into a short easy gully; the Megs Gill path is found just below it.

THE VIEW

The vale and village of Grasmere, seen in great detail, take pride of place in a very pleasing view, rich in lake scenery. There is good contrast between the sylvan beauty of the valleys of the Rothay and Brathay and the stark outline of the Coniston and Langdale fells.

This is probably as good a place as any for a newcomer to the district to appreciate its variety and unique charm.

Principal Fells

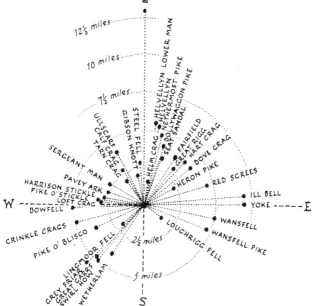

Lakes and Tarns

E: *Grasmere*
E: *Rydal Water*
SE: *Loughrigg Tarn*
SE: *Windermere (upper reach)*
S: *Coniston Water (small part)*

Walk 50 yards south of the cairn for a view of *Elter Water* (SSE)

RIDGE ROUTE

To LOUGHRIGG FELL, 1101': 2½ miles
S, then ESE, E and SE
Several depressions; main one 475'
850 feet of ascent
A very beautiful and easy walk,
finishing with a steep climb

SILVER HOW

1200

BLEA RIGG

LANGDALE

GRASMERE

900

800

ONE MILE

N

Spedding Crag

ruin

Cairn on rocky mound – viewpoint for Rydal and Grasmere

GRASMERE

GRASMERE

Red Bank

Loughrigg Terrace

500

600

700

800

1000

WALTHWAITE

Dow Bank

A branch path detours to the cairn on Spedding Crag, where there is a striking birds-eye view of Chapel Stile and Walthwaite

Dow Bank is the most prominent rise on the ridge

700

600

ELTERWATER

ELTERWATER

AMBLESIDE

LOUGHRIGG FELL

On merit, this should be a well-blazed route, for there are few more beautiful and interesting, but in fact for much of the way a narrow grass trod is the only guide. The views are delightful. Three passes between Grasmere and Langdale are crossed, the first the Megs Gill route, the second the Huntingstile route, and the well-known Red Bank road is the third. There should be no difficulty in mist.

Megs Gill

Cairn on the ridge overlooking Elter Water

RIDGE ROUTE

To BLEA RIGG, 1776': 2 miles
W, then WNW and N
A succession of little ups and downs
650 feet of ascent

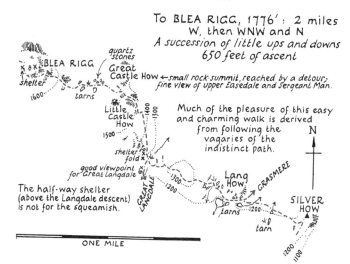

←*small rock summit, reached by a detour; fine view of upper Easedale and Sergeant Man.*

Much of the pleasure of this easy and charming walk is derived from following the vagaries of the indistinct path.

The half-way shelter (above the Langdale descent) is not for the squeamish.

ONE MILE

Langdale Pikes from the tarns below Lang How

9 Loughrigg Fell
from White Moss

Loughrigg Fell is one of the most varied fells in the Lake District, with things of interest and places to explore in abundance. It provides an exciting introduction to the fells for many walkers, and is a place that people tend to return to time after time. With its very modest height and easy climbing, it is also perfect for families seeking a short walk with plenty to keep children occupied.

As Wainwright points out in his notes, a climb of Loughrigg Fell gives views that are quite out of proportion to walkers' efforts. 'Of the lesser heights of Lakeland, Loughrigg Fell is pre-eminent... No ascent is more repaying for the small labour involved in visiting its many cairns.' The several subsidiary tops around the summit provide different views across the surrounding fells, lakes and tarns, while in between them are grassy hollows and slopes that children enjoy, and outcrops of rocks against which parents can lean back and enjoy the sights. Look out in particular for several of the other fells in this book, including Helm Crag and Silver How near Grasmere, Nab Scar on the Fairfield horseshoe, and Claife Heights. With so much to see in all directions and such a broad top to explore, Loughrigg Fell can feel like the very heart of the Lake District.

Unlike some other fells with terrific views, the routes up and down are just as good. This walk combines Wainwright's suggested ascents from White Moss and, coming down, Rydal, and they combine to reveal many of the fell's best features. The way up crosses some of the woodland that decorates the base of Loughrigg, before traversing the fell on one of the best trodden paths in the Lake District – Loughrigg Terrace. After that it is a short, sharp pull up to the top, which has a maze of paths because of its popularity, though the true summit, marked by a nice Ordnance Survey cairn, is obvious. The way back down takes in a lovely grassy bowl in the midst of the fell and, towards the bottom, the spectacular sight of Rydal Cave, a wide and deep reminder of the quarrying that once went on here.

Loughrigg – pronounced 'luffrigg' – is well worth exploring beyond this walk, and Wainwright's notes provide details of several more ascents to try. Each opens up a new side to the fell, which always rewards efforts to get to know it better. Loughrigg offers something for everyone.

From *Book Three: The Central Fells*

Distance 4 miles (6.4km)

Ascent 925 feet (280m)

Start and finish point The pay-and-display White Moss car park between Rydal and Grasmere (NY 348 065). See the note below on alternative parking

Ordnance Survey maps Explorer OL7; Landranger 90

Getting there

The White Moss car park is mid-way between Rydal and Grasmere off the A591. It is on the right as you drive from Rydal.

If it is full, there is another pay-and-display car park, also signposted as White Moss, a little way towards Rydal and Ambleside. From here, follow the footpath towards Grasmere to pick up the route. For free parking, continue beyond the suggested car park along the A591 in the direction of Grasmere for 55 yards (50m), then turn right up the hill. There are lay-bys for parking and, further up on the left, a small free car park. The walk back down, and up at the end of the walk, is steep but doesn't add much to the distance.

The start of the walk can be reached by the 555 bus, which runs between the north of the Lake District at Keswick and the south at Kendal. Ask the driver for the White Moss stop. To link things up to train services, head for Windermere on the Lakes Line and catch the 555 towards Keswick from the station.

Facilities, food and drink

Grasmere, a mile or so on from the car park, has plenty of options for eating and drinking, and so does Ambleside, a little further in the other direction. Ambleside also has the nearest tourist information centre, on Market Cross (0844 225 0544, www.thehubofambleside.co.uk).

In between the two is Rydal, and the Badger Bar at the Glen Rothay Hotel, right by the A591 as you drive from White Moss towards Ambleside, serves good homemade food and local beers (015394 34500, www.theglenrothay.co.uk). Turning off to the left just after here leads you past St Mary's Church up to Rydal Hall, now a Christian centre, though the gardens are open to all (015394 32050, www.rydalhall.org) and Rydal Mount, William Wordsworth's house for many years (015394 33002, www.rydalmount.co.uk). Both places have good tearooms, and the one at Rydal Hall is open every day except Christmas Day and has a box of books and toys for children.

Directions

1 Walk back to the main road from the car park, cross it with great care, and pass through a gap in the wall on the other side. Descend on some stone steps beyond. At a T-junction with a broader path, turn right. It winds along the River Rothay on the stretch that links the Rydal and Grasmere lakes, and reaches a long wooden footbridge. Do not cross this, but pass through the wooden gate ahead and continue along the track. After two more wooden gates, rise up through the wood, then drop down towards another wooden footbridge. Walk over this one, and on the other side (NY 344 059) continue ahead up the stone steps – but if you have time to spare, turn right to the 'beach' by Grasmere lake, a great spot for paddling and stone skimming.

2 At the junction of paths beyond the flight of steps, bear left. The path traverses the hillside and soon picks up a dry stone wall to your left. Follow this until the wall meets a

junction with another, and here turn sharp right to traverse the hillside again. It involves doubling back on yourself, but it reduces the sharpness of the ascent. This is now Loughrigg Terrace, a broad path with tremendous views over Grasmere lake and the fells beyond. Follow it to a wall running across your path in front of a stream and wood, where you turn sharp left up stone steps set into the grass. The climb is steeper now, and continues along a very clear path, with more stretches of stone steps, right up to the Ordnance Survey column on the summit of Loughrigg Fell (NY 347 051).

3 Head south-east from the cairn, down to a pile of stones in a grassy depression. (You can divert to the right here for one of the fell's alternative summits, which has views down to Loughrigg Tarn.) Carry on past the stones and soon descend on another flight of stone steps. Just beyond the bottom of these, bear left on a grassy path that leads up to a small marshy tarn. Carry on along the path to descend to a wide grassy bowl, described by Wainwright as an amphitheatre. It can be boggy after heavy rain. The path continues over the amphitheatre and soon brings Rydal Water into view ahead. When you reach a grassy viewpoint over to the lake, the path bears slightly left, towards the left-hand side of some trees by the lake. Further down it meets some disused quarries, with spectacular Rydal Cave to the left (NY 355 058).

4 Continue on past the cave – the route diverts from Wainwright's suggestions here – and traverse the fellside on the high path, with Rydal Water down to your right. It leads up to the junction of paths followed earlier. Take the right-hand fork to descend. Just over 165 yards (150m) on, fork right at another junction. After another 110 yards (100m), it enters White Moss Wood at a kissing gate. The path now winds down on the other side of the River Rothay from earlier, later crossing it on a wooden footbridge. On the other side, walk back up to the road along the track, path and steps followed earlier, then cross carefully for the car park.

Loughrigg Fell

1101'

more often referred to
simply as 'Loughrigg'
(pronounced Lúffrigg)

• Grasmere

SILVER
▲ HOW   • Rydal

▲
LOUGHRIGG FELL   • Ambleside

•   • Clappersgate
Skelwith Bridge

MILES

0   1   2   3   4

from Mandale Bridge
(near Skelwith Bridge)

NATURAL FEATURES

Of the lesser heights of Lakeland, Loughrigg Fell is pre-eminent. It has no pretensions to mountain form, being a sprawling, ill-shaped wedge of rough country rising between the park-like valleys of Brathay and Rothay, and having a bulk out of all proportion to its modest altitude; but no ascent is more repaying for the small labour involved in visiting its many cairns, for Loughrigg has delightful grassy paths, a series of pleasant surprises along the traverse of the summits, several charming vistas and magnificent views, fine contrasts of velvety turf, rich bracken and grey rock, a string of little tarns like pearls in a necklace, and a wealth of stately trees on the flanks. It is especially well endowed with lakes, with four sheets of water, all lovely, touching its lower slopes, and in addition it nurses a large tarn to which it gives its name — and this is a distinction not attained by any other fell. It has also more paths to the square mile than any other fell, great or small, and amongst them is one that far exceeds in popularity any other in the district, one that all visitors know: Loughrigg Terrace. Short crags on every flank offer excellent sport for the rock-scrambler. Woodlands surround the base of the fell and creep up the slopes; higher, juniper, holly and yew straggle the fellside. Loughrigg has yet another attraction in the form of a tremendous cave, big enough to contain the entire population of Ambleside, which, although manmade and now disused, is still a remarkable place. In brief, this fell has a wealth of interests and delights, and for many people who now find pleasure in walking over the greater mountains it served as an introduction and an inspiration. Everybody likes Loughrigg.

Topographically, Loughrigg Fell is the corner-stone of the high mass of land lying south-west of the Rothay valley system, with High Raise as the loftiest point, but is almost isolated, the connecting link being a low and indefinite ridge crossed by the Red Bank road between Grasmere and Langdale. The fell, two miles long, has subsidiary summits overlooking each of the surrounding lakes.

MAP

There are two car
parks by the main road
at White Moss Common.

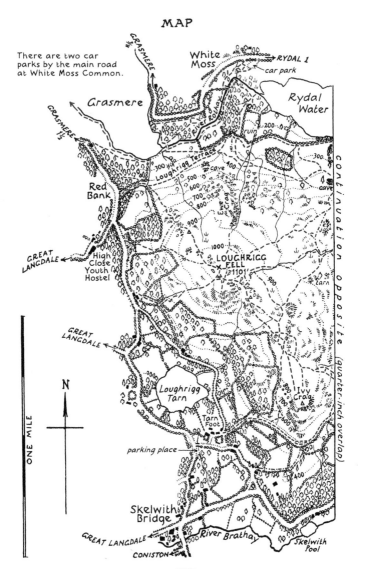

ONE MILE

N

MAP

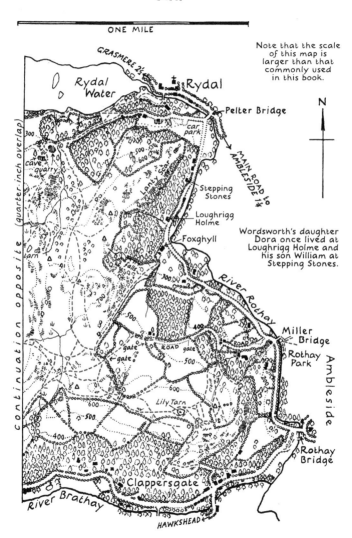

ONE MILE

Note that the scale of this map is larger than that commonly used in this book.

GRASMERE 2½

Rydal Water

Rydal

Pelter Bridge

car park

MAIN ROAD TO AMBLESIDE 1¾

N

300

cave quarry

Loughrigg Scar

Stepping Stones

Loughrigg Holme

Foxghyll

Wordsworth's daughter Dora once lived at Loughrigg Holme and his son William at Stepping Stones.

tarn

700

River Rothay

500

300

500

Miller Bridge

gate

400

Rothay Park

gate

ROAD

gate

Ambleside

600

500

Lily Tarn

600

500

400

Rothay Bridge

Clappersgate

River Brathay

HAWKSHEAD

continuation opposite (quarter-inch overlap)

103

ASCENTS

When fellwalking, it is better to arrive than to travel hopefully and this is justification for the inclusion here of six pages of directions for reaching the summit of Loughrigg Fell, because, although of insignificant altitude, the fell has an extensive and confusing top, the ultimate objective remains hidden on the approach, and the maze of paths needs careful unravelling — besides, failure would be *too* humiliating! On a first visit it is not only not easy to locate the highest point amongst the score of likely-looking protuberances several of which carry likely-looking cairns, it is actually difficult not to go astray, and, in mist, positively easy to do so.

ASCENT FROM GRASMERE
920 feet of ascent : 2¼ miles

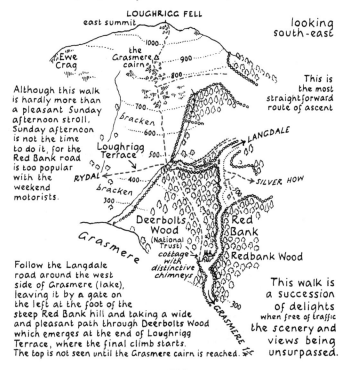

LOUGHRIGG FELL

east summit

looking south-east

Ewe Crag

the Grasmere cairn

1000...

900

800

This is the most straightforward route of ascent

Although this walk is hardly more than a pleasant Sunday afternoon stroll, Sunday afternoon is not the time to do it, for the Red Bank road is too popular with the weekend motorists.

700...

bracken

600...

500...

400...

300

Loughrigg Terrace

RYDAL

bracken

LANGDALE

SILVER HOW

Deerbolts Wood (National Trust)

cottage with distinctive chimneys

Red Bank

Redbank Wood

Grasmere

300

GRASMERE

Follow the Langdale road around the west side of Grasmere (lake), leaving it by a gate on the left at the foot of the steep Red Bank hill and taking a wide and pleasant path through Deerbolts Wood which emerges at the end of Loughrigg Terrace, where the final climb starts. The top is not seen until the Grasmere cairn is reached.

This walk is a succession of delights when free of traffic the scenery and views being unsurpassed.

ASCENT FROM AMBLESIDE
1050 feet of ascent : 2½ miles

LOUGHRIGG FELL

south summit

east summit

viewpoint for Loughrigg Tarn

Ivy Crag

good viewpoint for Windermere

1000

tarns

tarns

900

bracken

800

bracken

700

600

SKELWITH BRIDGE

tarn

RYDAL

Troughton Gill

A stands for Amphitheatre
— a shallow depression, once
used as a rifle range and
now a meeting-place
of many paths

gate

600

former golf course
(club disbanded 1956
— lack of support)

former clubhouse
(now private
residence)

gate

500

400

Juniper

gate

300

TODD CRAG

400

stile

Brow Head
Farm

private
grounds

Foxghyll

signpost

RYDAL

300

Loughrigg
Brow

ROAD

private grounds

200

Fox
How

looking west

unusual wall
of stone slabs

River Rothay

ROTHAY
BRIDGE ½

Miller Bridge

Foxghyll was once
the home of Thomas de
Quincey, and Fox How was
owned by Matthew Arnold.

Rothay
Park

useful little
building

St. Mary's
Church

school

Ambleside

A beautiful walk, to be done
leisurely. The usual route
is by way of Brow Head Farm
but the path from Foxghyll
has, initially, an intimate
charm all its own, although
inferior in views.

ASCENT FROM RYDAL
1000 feet of ascent : 2½ miles

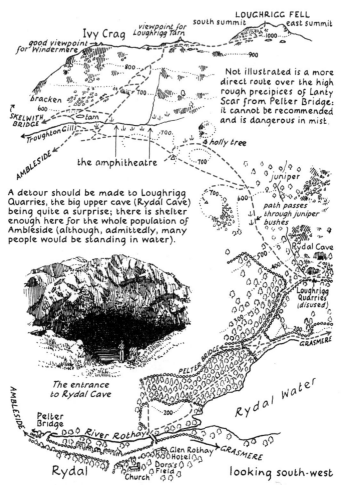

LOUGHRIGG FELL
south summit
east summit
viewpoint for Loughrigg Tarn
Ivy Crag
good viewpoint
for Windermere
bracken
SKELWITH BRIDGE
tarn
Troughton Gill
AMBLESIDE
the amphitheatre
holly tree

Not illustrated is a more
direct route over the high
rough precipices of Lanty
Scar from Pelter Bridge:
it cannot be recommended
and is dangerous in mist.

juniper
path passes
through juniper
bushes
Rydal Cave
Loughrigg
Quarries
(disused)
GRASMERE

A detour should be made to Loughrigg
Quarries, the big upper cave (Rydal Cave)
being quite a surprise; there is shelter
enough here for the whole population of
Ambleside (although, admittedly, many
people would be standing in water).

*The entrance
to Rydal Cave*

PELTER BRIDGE
AMBLESIDE
Pelter
Bridge
River Rothay
Rydal
Church
Dora's
Field
Glen Rothay
Hotel
GRASMERE
Rydal Water

looking south-west

There is no better introduction to the manifold attractions
of Loughrigg Fell than this easy and delightful approach.

ASCENT FROM WHITE MOSS
925 feet of ascent : 1½ miles

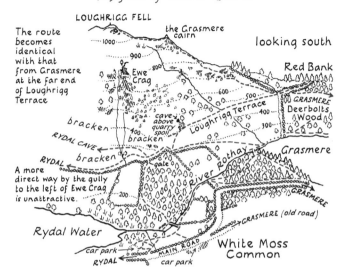

The route becomes identical with that from Grasmere at the far end of Loughrigg Terrace

LOUGHRIGG FELL

the Grasmere cairn

looking south

1000

900

Ewe Crag

600

500

400

300

Red Bank

GRASMERE Deerbolts Wood

bracken

RYDAL CAVE

RYDAL

bracken

cave above quarry spoil

bracken

400

Loughrigg Terrace

Grasmere

A more direct way by the gully to the left of Ewe Crag is unattractive.

200

gate

River Rothay

GRASMERE

GRASMERE (old road)

Rydal Water

car park

RYDAL

MAIN ROAD

car park

White Moss Common

This might be described as 'the motorist's route', not because it is practicable for cars (!) but because there are two popular car parks beside the main road at White Moss Common.

Grasmere
from Loughrigg Terrace

ASCENT FROM CLAPPERSGATE
1050 feet of ascent : 2½ miles

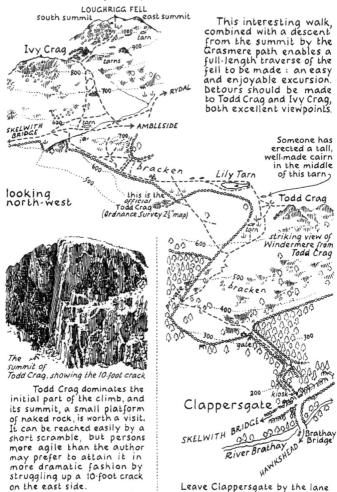

This interesting walk, combined with a descent from the summit by the Grasmere path enables a full-length traverse of the fell to be made : an easy and enjoyable excursion. Detours should be made to Todd Crag and Ivy Crag, both excellent viewpoints.

Someone has erected a tall, well-made cairn in the middle of this tarn

striking view of Windermere from Todd Crag

The summit of Todd Crag, showing the 10-foot crack

Todd Crag dominates the initial part of the climb, and its summit, a small platform of naked rock, is worth a visit. It can be reached easily by a short scramble, but persons more agile than the author may prefer to attain it in more dramatic fashion by struggling up a 10-foot crack on the east side.

Similar rocky heights nearby are also interesting.

Leave Clappersgate by the lane directly opposite the road junction.

108

ASCENT FROM SKELWITH BRIDGE
1000 feet of ascent: 1¼ miles

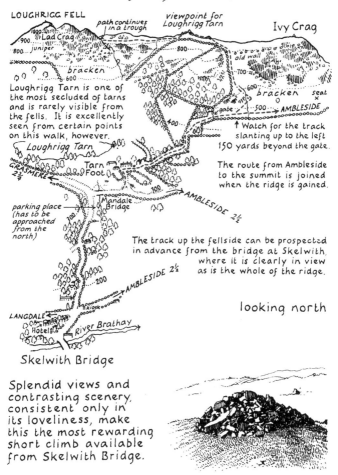

LOUGHRIGG FELL

path continues in a trough

viewpoint for Loughrigg Tarn

Ivy Crag

1000
900
800
Lad Crag
Juniper

800

old wall
700

bracken
600

bracken   seat

Loughrigg Tarn is one of the most secluded of tarns and is rarely visible from the fells. It is excellently seen from certain points on this walk, however.

gate   500   AMBLESIDE

400

↑ Watch for the track slanting up to the left 150 yards beyond the gate.

Loughrigg Tarn

Tarn Foot

GRASMERE 2¼

300

AMBLESIDE 2¼

The route from Ambleside to the summit is joined when the ridge is gained.

parking place (has to be approached from the north)

Mandale Bridge

The track up the fellside can be prospected in advance from the bridge at Skelwith, where it is clearly in view as is the whole of the ridge.

200

AMBLESIDE 2½

looking north

LANGDALE

kiosk

Hotels

River Brathay

Skelwith Bridge

Splendid views and contrasting scenery, consistent only in its loveliness, make this the most rewarding short climb available from Skelwith Bridge.

The cairn on Ivy Crag
a good viewpoint for Windermere and Langdale, reached by a simple detour along the ridge.

THE SUMMIT

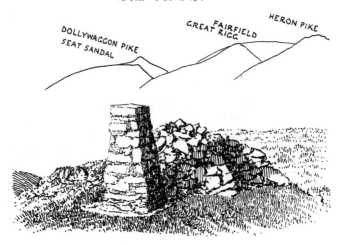

Three eminences rise close together above the undulating top of the fell, and the middle one, slightly higher than the other two, bears an Ordnance Survey triangulation column that the surveyors who built it, after building so many, must have voted the most beautifully situated of all. It is starting to crumble. The small area of the principal summit is carpeted with a velvety turf. There are several tarns, little more than dewponds, in the green hollows around. These tend to dry up in the summer. Bracken encroaches in patches on the higher parts of the fell and, especially in winter, make the summit a colourful place.

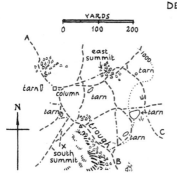

DESCENTS : There are hundreds of rocky tors and low crags scattered about the fell top and descents are most easily made by using the paths, of which there is also a great abundance. The quickest way down (and the best in mist) is by the Grasmere route to Loughrigg Terrace.

A : to Grasmere and Loughrigg Terrace
B : to Ambleside, Clappersgate Rydal and Skelwith Bridge
C : an alternative to B (joins it in a further quarter-mile)

RIDGE ROUTE

**To SILVER HOW, 1292′ : 2½ miles
NW, then W, WNW and N
Several depressions ; main one 475′
950 feet of ascent
A sharp descent is followed by
a beautiful and easy walk**

SILVER HOW

1200

BLEA RIGG

LANGDALE

1000

GRASMERE

900

800

Spedding Crag

WALTHWAITE

Dow Bank

At this col, climb half-right between low crags

Viewpoint for Rydal and ruin Grasmere

GRASMERE

GRASMERE

GRASMERE

N

HALF A MILE

Red Bank

Loughrigg Terrace

500

600

700

700

600

800

900

1000

LOUGHRIGG FELL ×

ELTERWATER

ELTERWATER

AMBLESIDE

Make the little detour to the cairn on Spedding Crag, where there is a striking birds-eye view of Chapel Stile and Walthwaite.

Dow Bank is the most prominent rise on the ridge, the climb to it being steep.

This pleasant stroll is full of interest and variety : it has lake and woodland scenes, rocky outcrops, a few yards of macadam(!) and its gentle undulations are crossed by favourite paths from Grasmere to Langdale. The views are delightful on all sides. In bad weather do not proceed beyond the final col unless the ground is well known ; paths on Silver How are a source of trouble in mist.

Loughrigg Tarn

Loughrigg Fell 13

THE VIEW

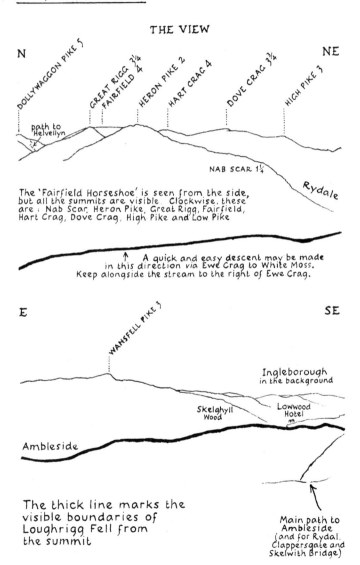

N

DOLLYWAGGON PIKE 5

GREAT RIGG 2¼
FAIRFIELD 4

HERON PIKE 2

HART CRAG 4

DOVE CRAG 3¾

HIGH PIKE 3

NE

path to Helvellyn

NAB SCAR 1¼

Rydale

The 'Fairfield Horseshoe' is seen from the side, but all the summits are visible. Clockwise, these are : Nab Scar, Heron Pike, Great Rigg, Fairfield, Hart Crag, Dove Crag, High Pike and Low Pike

↑ A quick and easy descent may be made in this direction via Ewe Crag to White Moss. Keep alongside the stream to the right of Ewe Crag.

E

WANSFELL PIKE 3

SE

Ingleborough in the background

Skelghyll Wood

Lowwood Hotel

Ambleside

The thick line marks the visible boundaries of Loughrigg Fell from the summit

Main path to Ambleside (and for Rydal, Clappersgate and Skelwith Bridge)

THE VIEW

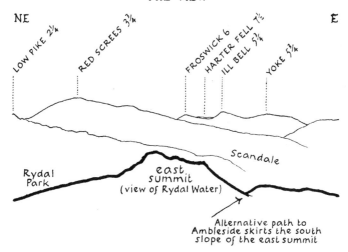

NE

LOW PIKE 2¼
RED SCREES 3¾
FROSWICK 6
HARTER FELL 7½
ILL BELL 5¾
YOKE 5¾

E

Scandale

Rydal Park

east summit
(view of Rydal Water)

Alternative path to
Ambleside skirts the south
slope of the east summit

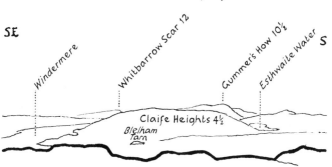

SE

Windermere
Whitbarrow Scar 12
Gummer's How 10½
Esthwaite Water

S

Claife Heights 4½

Blelham Tarn

south summit
(view of Loughrigg Tarn)

In addition to the triple main summit
the tops of Todd Crag and Ivy Crag are
also excellent viewpoints, presenting new
scenes, and they should be visited for a
more comprehensive study of the surrounding
district. Todd Crag has a surprising view of
Windermere, Ivy Crag a beautiful one of the
Brathay Valley leading to Great Langdale

The figures following the names of fells indicate distances in miles

THE VIEW

Anybody spending a first holiday in Ambleside cannot do better than make an early visit to the top of Loughrigg Fell. From this elevation he will get an excellent idea of the topography of the neighbourhood, all the fells and valleys within easy reach being attractively displayed. He will see around him a land very rich in promise — and find it even richer in fulfilment. The following fellwalks suggest themselves for a week's stay: I – THE FAIRFIELD HORSESHOE; 2 – THE CONISTON FELLS (ridgewalk, Wetherlam to Old Man) 3 – BOWFELL and CRINKLE CRAGS; 4 – HARRISON STICKLE, SERGEANT MAN and the SILVER HOW ridge; 5 – THE EASEDALE FELLS (circuit of Far Easedale) 6 – DOLLYWAGGON PIKE and HELVELLYN. Of course the separate ascents of RED SCREES and WANSFELL PIKE cannot possibly be omitted — if time is short, these two climbs should be done before breakfast (best part of the day for fellwalking) on the day of departure. A better plan, however, is to stay on for another week, for the suggested itinerary by no means exhausts the area's attractions.

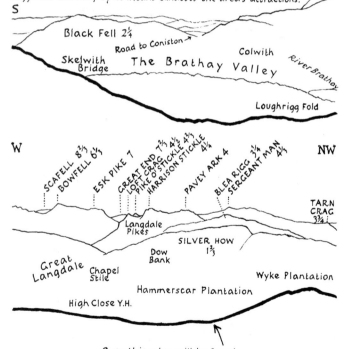

Over this edge will be found an intermittent path that goes down (between walls) to the road near the grounds of High Close.

THE VIEW

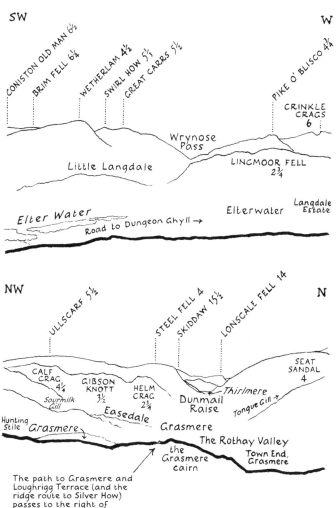

The path to Grasmere and
Loughrigg Terrace (and the
ridge route to Silver How)
passes to the right of
the Grasmere cairn.

10 Lingmoor Fell
from The Old Dungeon Ghyll, Great Langdale

The Langdale valley has much grander peaks than Lingmoor Fell, but none is as well suited to families as this, and few can match the panoramic views from the top. While visitors pour down the valley to climb the Langdale Pikes on the northern side, far fewer turn south, and even on busy summer days you will get plenty of space to yourselves here.

This route up Lingmoor Fell starts at the Old Dungeon Ghyll Hotel, one of the unofficial headquarters of Lake District walking – the kind of place where weather-beaten hikers and climbers gather to swap stories of their days on the fells over a pint – and a good base for families too. The climb up is steady and easy underfoot, and passes over the heather-covered slopes that give Lingmoor Fell its name. The way up does not include the fell's craggy subsidiary, Side Pike, though anyone wanting to add that in can take a detour to it at the point, about halfway up, marked in the directions.

Lingmoor Fell stands gloriously separate and distinct in the Langdale valley, so the views from the top are magnificent all round, taking in fells including the Langdale Pikes and several lakes and tarns, too. The way down has more great views over the valley, and passes by Blea Tarn and a remote house of the same name, referenced by William Wordsworth in 'The Solitary' section of his epic poem *The Excursion*: 'Beneath our feet, a little lowly vale / A lowly vale, and yet uplifted high / Among the mountains . . . / A liquid pool that glittered in the sun / And one bare dwelling; one abode, no more!'

This is a wonderful walk, described by Wainwright as an ideal one 'for an easy first day of a Langdale holiday', but in fact worthy of a family excursion on any given day. Look out too for three of the things that make the Lake District's fells so distinctive: Herdwick sheep, which have grazed here for centuries; the remnants of quarries, which have turned out elegant green slate for just as long, though these are mostly on the other side; and dry stone walls. The wall here clings to the fell's spine and remains intact for much of its length, its piled stones miraculously clinging to the sharp contours in testament to the skills of the hardy men who built it.

From *Book Four: The Southern Fells*

Distance 4 miles (6.4km)

Ascent 1,250 feet (380m)

Start and finish point The National Trust pay-and-display car park at the Old Dungeon Ghyll Hotel in Great Langdale (NY 286 061). It is free for National Trust members

Ordnance Survey maps Explorer OL6; Landranger 90

Getting there
The Old Dungeon Ghyll is at the very end of the B5343, a winding but delightful road from Skelwith Bridge, which in turn is connected to Ambleside and Coniston by the A593. From the west, Langdale is reached by the Hardknott and Wrynose Passes, spectacular roads through the heights of the fells that are not for the faint-hearted, and not to be recommended at all in bad weather. Once at the Old Dungeon Ghyll, follow the signs for the public car park area, as some of it is for hotel residents only.

The 516 bus – the Langdale Rambler – stops right by the Old Dungeon Ghyll Hotel and connects you with Ambleside, Skelwith Bridge, Elterwater and Chapel Stile. It only runs four to six times a day, so check times carefully before you plan a journey.

Facilities, food and drink
The Old Dungeon Ghyll Hotel has a popular Hikers' Bar that is child and muddy boot-friendly, and there are tables outside

to enjoy the views on warmer days (015394 37272, www.odg.co.uk). A mile back down the Langdale valley is the New Dungeon Ghyll Hotel, which also has a bar for walkers and welcomes children and dogs (015394 37213, www.dungeon-ghyll.co.uk). Both hotels have comfortable rooms to stay.

Chapel Stile has the nearest shop, open seven days a week and stocking lots of local products and camping essentials. It also hosts the Brambles Café (015394 37500) and the Langdale complex of hotel, pub – named Wainwrights' Inn in honour of the great man – self-catering apartments and spa (015394 38088, www.langdale.co.uk). Also recommended for food and drink further back up the valley are the Britannia Inn in Elterwater (015394 37210, www.britinn.net) and the café–restaurant Chesters at Skelwith Bridge (015394 34711, www.chestersbytheriver.co.uk).

Directions

1 Walk back to the road from the car park. Turn right and follow the road, which soon bends to the left by a red post-box. Where it bends to the right, just after crossing a stream, leave it to the left through a wooden gate, signposted for Side Pike and Lingmoor Fell. Walk through the car parking area ahead with a wall close by on your right for about 55 yards (50m), then leave it to your right to cross a small wooden footbridge.

2 Follow this stony path to pass through two more wooden gates in quick succession, then cross a field to another gate and rise up between trees to another. The path now climbs steadily upwards, with a wall close by on your right and, further up, a road on the other side of it, and eventually reaches a gate leading on to the road (NY 289 051).

3 (If you want to add Side Pike to the walk, turn left here and climb up to the rocky summit, about ¼ mile (400m) away. But be warned that it requires a bit of scrambling, and the sheer drops make it unsuitable for small children. Descending by

the other side is not recommended either, so return by the way you went up.) Continue on from the gate, crossing half left to another one, which leads on to a path traversing the hillside through bracken. After crossing a stile in a fence, the path turns left to climb steeply up, with Side Pike over the fence to your left. Where the path meets a wall, turn right to follow it.

4 The path now rises with the wall, with bracken giving way to heather on the slopes. At a gap in the wall, the path crosses to the other side of it via a stile, and now continues with the wall on your right. Where the wall becomes broken and is joined by a fence, the path bends right and continues to follow it all the way to the top of Lingmoor Fell, called Brown How and marked by a small cairn on top of a mound a few steps from a stile in the fence (NY 303 046).

5 Cross the stile to continue ahead, the wall and fence again to your right. Descend to a hollow with some trees, and cross the wall via a stile. The path now bends away from the wall and descends, with the distinctive Langdale Pikes soon visible ahead, as well as Blea Tarn on the floor of the valley. After passing through a gap in a wall, the path drops down to the road. Turn right, immediately passing Bleatarn House (NY 296 048).

6 After about 325 yards (300m), look out for a signpost on the right indicating the public footpath for Side Pike. Follow the path up for about 75 yards (70m), then turn left over a stile – this is the traverse of Side Pike followed earlier in the other direction. It reaches the gate by the road and the signpost for Side Pike. For variety, you could join the road as it winds down to the Old Dungeon Ghyll, though the footpath is much nicer and more direct. Follow the path with the wall on your left, down to the succession of wooden gates, and back at the road turn right for the Old Dungeon Ghyll car park.

Lingmoor Fell

1539'

from Elter Water

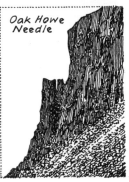

Oak Howe Needle

Dungeon Ghyll
● (Old Hotel)

Chapel Stile ●

LINGMOOR ▲
FELL   Elterwater ●

Fell Foot ●   ● Little
                  Langdale

MILES

0   1   2

NATURAL FEATURES

A crescent-shaped ridge of high ground rises to the west from Elterwater's pleasant pastures, climbs to a well-defined summit, a fine vantage point, and then curves northwards as it descends to valley-level near Dungeon Ghyll. Within the crescent lies Great Langdale, the longer outside curve sloping down into Little Langdale and the Blea Tarn depression. The mass is Lingmoor Fell, so named because of the extensive zone of heather clothing the northern flanks below the summit. The fell has contributed generously to the prosperity of the surrounding valleys, for not only has it nurtured the sheep but it has also been quarried extensively for many generations, yielding a very beautiful and durable green stone. Bracken and heather, some ragged patches of juniper and well-timbered estate woods, many crags and a delectable little tarn, all combine to make this fell a colourful addition to the varied attractions of the Langdale area.

looking west

1 : The summit
2 : Side Pike
3 : Oakhowe Crag
4 : Oak Howe Needle
5 : Bield Crag
6 : Sawrey's Wood
7 : Baysbrown Wood
8 : Elter Water
9 : Little Langdale Tarn
10 : Lingmoor Tarn
11 : Great Langdale Beck
12 : River Brathay
13 : Bleamoss Beck
14 : Great Langdale
15 : Little Langdale

MAP

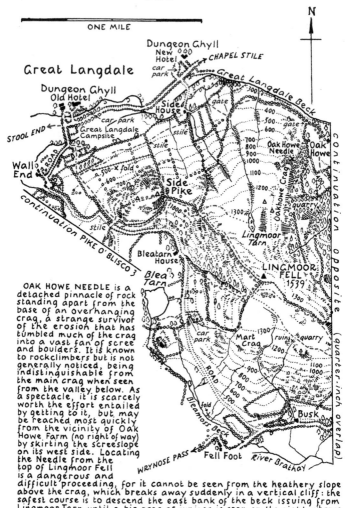

ONE MILE

N

Dungeon Ghyll
New Hotel
car park
CHAPEL STILE

Great Langdale

Dungeon Ghyll
Old Hotel

STOOL END ←

car park

Great Langdale Campsite

Side House

gate

Great Langdale Beck

stile

300
400
500
600

gate

700
800
900
1000

Oak Howe Needle

Oak Howe

1100

Wall End

500
600
700

x fold

1200

Oakhowe Crag

quarry

Side Pike

1100

stile

1300

Lingmoor Tarn

LINGMOOR FELL
1539'

Bleatarn House

Blea Tarn

1300

car park

Mart Crag

ruins
quarry

1300
1200

900
800
700
600
500

1100
1000

Busk

fold

Bleamoss Beck

WRYNOSE PASS

Fell Foot

River Brathay

continuation PIKE O'BLISCO 3

continuation opposite (quarter-inch overlap)

OAK HOWE NEEDLE is a detached pinnacle of rock standing apart from the base of an overhanging crag, a strange survivor of the erosion that has tumbled much of the crag into a vast fan of scree and boulders. It is known to rockclimbers but is not generally noticed, being indistinguishable from the main crag when seen from the valley below. As a spectacle, it is scarcely worth the effort entailed by getting to it, but may be reached most quickly from the vicinity of Oak Howe Farm (no right of way) by skirting the screeslope on its west side. Locating the Needle from the top of Lingmoor Fell is a dangerous and difficult proceeding, for it cannot be seen from the heathery slope above the crag, which breaks away suddenly in a vertical cliff: the safest course is to descend the east bank of the beck issuing from Lingmoor Tarn until a big area of juniper is seen on the right, whence by walking eastwards above it, a small bracken col is reached —— and there, directly in front and quite close, is Oak Howe Needle.

MAP

Great Langdale is probably the most frequented valley in the district, with a heavy inflow of visitors summer and winter alike, most of them bound for Dungeon Ghyll. In former years the whole of the traffic, both on foot and awheel, was confined to the one road in the valley, on the north side, while the south side, along the base of Lingmoor Fell, seldom saw a soul. In 1960 the author commented on this and said how much pleasanter it would be if there were public rights of way linking Baysbrown, Oak Howe, Side House and Wall End. Today there is a public bridleway from Baysbrown to Oak Howe, a public footpath from Oak Howe to Side House, and a permitted footpath from Side House to within a quarter of a mile of Wall End.

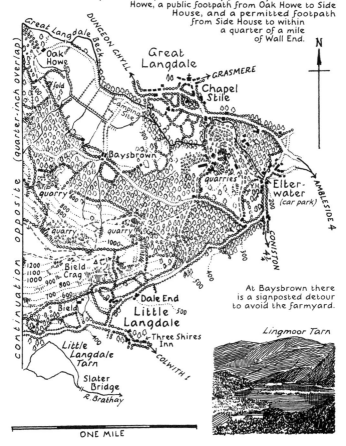

At Baysbrown there is a signposted detour to avoid the farmyard.

Lingmoor Tarn

ONE MILE

ASCENT FROM DUNGEON GHYLL
1250 feet of ascent : 2 miles
(Add 250 feet and ½ mile if Side Pike is included)

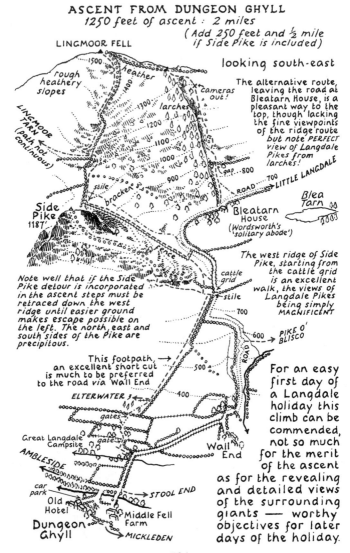

LINGMOOR FELL

rough heathery slopes

1500

heather

1400

Cameras out!

1300

larches

1200

1100

1000

900

gap 800

LINGMOOR TARN (path not continuous)

stile

bracken

Side Pike 1187'

fence

looking south-east

The alternative route, leaving the road at Bleatarn House, is a pleasant way to the top, though lacking the fine viewpoints of the ridge route but note *PERFECT view of Langdale Pikes from larches!*

ROAD 700 **LITTLE LANGDALE**

Blea Tarn

Bleatarn House (Wordsworth's 'solitary abode')

The west ridge of Side Pike, starting from the cattle grid is an excellent walk, the views of Langdale Pikes being simply MAGNIFICENT

cattle grid

stile

700

Note well that if the Side Pike detour is incorporated in the ascent steps must be retraced down the west ridge until easier ground makes escape possible on the left. The north, east and south sides of the Pike are precipitous.

600 **PIKE O' BLISCO**

ROAD

This footpath, an excellent short cut is much to be preferred to the road via Wall End

500

400

ELTERWATER 3

gates

Great Langdale Campsite

gate

AMBLESIDE

car park

Wall End

Old Hotel

STOOL END

Middle Fell Farm

Dungeon Ghyll

MICKLEDEN

For an easy first day of a Langdale holiday this climb can be commended, not so much for the merit of the ascent as for the revealing and detailed views of the surrounding giants — worthy objectives for later days of the holiday.

Side Pike
from the ridge
running up to
Lingmoor Fell

Side Pike is accessible to the walker by its west ridge only, and there is no other safe way off. When descending from the cairn do not be tempted by a track going down eastwards: this ends suddenly above a vertical drop, with easy ground tantalisingly close, *but out of reach*. On the drawing above, this dangerous trap is seen directly below the X.

Langdale Pikes
from Side Pike
1: Pike o' Stickle
2: Loft Crag
3: Thorn Crag
4: Harrison
   Stickle
5: Pavey Ark

ASCENTS FROM ELTERWATER AND CHAPEL STILE
1350 feet of ascent : 2½ miles

When the ridge wall is reached, climb over the gate and follow the wall to the right. The wall is not continuous to the summit. *The edge of the top quarry is unprotected and dangerous.*

LINGMOOR FELL

1500
1400
1300
1200
1100
1000

quarries

gate with steps
1000

900

prominent yew — Watch for sharp turn left when opposite to it

If the route from the gate on the road is taken, watch for the indistinct bifurcation left, passing through a gate in the fence.

LITTLE LANGDALE ½

800

juniper

700

bracken

quarries

From this section of the path, Oak Howe Needle is clearly in view (to the right) standing apart from the base of a crag.

500

gate

cave

500

From Elterwater it is a simpler plan to by-pass the lower quarries by using one of the two routes leaving the upper Little Langdale road

Baysbrown Wood
400

BAYSBROWN ½

Sawrey's Wood

Baysbrown Estate

400

store ground spoil heaps

Great Langdale Beck

DUNGEON GHYLL 2

300

quarries

steps

CONISTON 4

Chapel Stile

GRASMERE 3

Youth Hostel
car park
200

Langdale Estate
Britannia Inn

looking west-south-west

AMBLESIDE 4

Elterwater

AMBLESIDE 4

The lower quarries are a labyrinth of paths and cart-tracks, confusing on a first visit. The extensive spoil-heaps are not pretty, the many trees being an ineffective screen; nevertheless, this is an interesting and attractive approach to the ridge.

ASCENT FROM LITTLE LANGDALE
1100 feet of ascent :
1½ miles (from Dale End)

LINGMOOR FELL

The quarry track may be followed (easy walking) to its terminus at some ruins, disused workings, whence the same direction may be continued along a shallow trough to join the Bleatarn House route at a wall. Or the track may be left when it turns towards the ridge-wall beyond the big cairn above Bield Crag, and the ridge then followed to the top. Watch for the junction or it will be missed.

heather
1400
grass
1300
ruins
1400
1300
1200
ruin
quarries ✕ ruins

The edge of this quarry is unprotected and dangerous.

→ CHAPEL STILE and ELTERWATER

Bield Crag

1000

Little Langdale

WRYNOSE PASS and BLEATARN

Bield
700
bracken
gate

Dale End
gate
gate
600
↑ Three Shires Inn
looking west

A grassy quarry track serves excellently to point the way and ease the journey. On this route the best views remain hidden until the moment of arrival at the summit.

COLWITH →
← ELTERWATER ¾

THE SUMMIT

The highest point, adjacent to an angle in the summit wall, is a stony mound superimposed on a dome dark with heather (Brown How), and owns a large cairn. 150 yards east, along the line of a fence, are the remains of a second cairn, a good viewpoint.
DESCENTS: Routes of ascent may be reversed, with the old wall as guide initially. *In mist,* when descending the south-east ridge, care should be taken to skirt the quarry and not fall into it — many people have had a shock here.

The Coniston Fells

WETHERLAM   SWIRL   GREAT
                    HOW   CARRS

RIDGE ROUTES : Lingmoor Fell is isolated from other fells and therefore has no connecting ridges. Its nearest neighbour is Pike o' Blisco, but the considerable descent to the Bleatarn road makes a climb therefrom virtually a complete ascent.

THE VIEW

looking north-west

1 : Pike o' Stickle   2 : Loft Crag   3 : Thorn Crag
4 : Harrison Stickle   5 : Pavey Ark   6 : High Raise
7 : Sergeant Man   8 : Gimmer Crag   9 : Dungeon Ghyll
10 : Stickle Ghyll   11 : Tarn Crag   12 : Middlefell Buttress
13 : Pike Howe

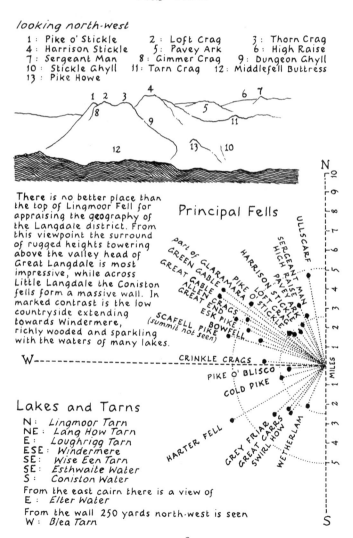

There is no better place than the top of Lingmoor Fell for appraising the geography of the Langdale district. From this viewpoint the surround of rugged heights towering above the valley head of Great Langdale is most impressive, while across Little Langdale the Coniston fells form a massive wall. In marked contrast is the low countryside extending towards Windermere, richly wooded and sparkling with the waters of many lakes.

Principal Fells

Lakes and Tarns

N : Lingmoor Tarn
NE : Lang How Tarn
E : Loughrigg Tarn
ESE : Windermere
SE : Wise Een Tarn
SE : Esthwaite Water
S : Coniston Water

From the east cairn there is a view of
E : Elter Water

From the wall 250 yards north-west is seen
W : Blea Tarn

128

THE VIEW

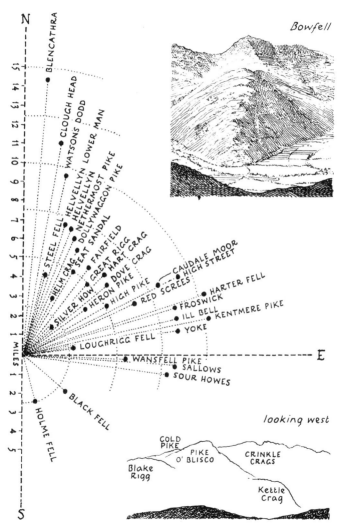

Bowfell

N

15
14
13
12
11
10
9
8
7
6
5
4
3
2
1

MILES

1
2
3
4
5

S

E

BLENCATHRA
CLOUGH HEAD
WATSONS DODD
HELVELLYN LOWER MAN
HELVELLYN
NETHERMOST PIKE
STEEL FELL
DOLLYWAGGON PIKE
SEAT SANDAL
HELM CRAG
FAIRFIELD
GREAT RIGG
SILVER HOW
HART CRAG
DOVE CRAG
HERON PIKE
HIGH PIKE
CAUDALE MOOR
HIGH STREET
RED SCREES
HARTER FELL
FROSWICK
ILL BELL
KENTMERE PIKE
LOUGHRIGG FELL
YOKE
WANSFELL PIKE
SALLOWS
SOUR HOWES
BLACK FELL
HOLME FELL

looking west

COLD PIKE
PIKE O' BLISCO
CRINKLE CRAGS
Blake Rigg
Kettle Crag

129

11 Holme Fell
from Tarn Hows

The abundance of pretty tarns is one of the things that makes the Lake District so distinctive, and this walk combines a fell climb with one of its most attractive and popular – Tarn Hows.

Tarn Hows is actually an artificial lake, but one made with great sensitivity. The area was once made up of several smaller tarns with surrounding marshy land, but was reconfigured by landowners in the late nineteenth century with the construction of a dam that flooded the area into the current tarn and the planting of many more trees around it. The area was bought by Beatrix Potter in the 1930s, and bequeathed by her to the National Trust, which continues to look after it today. Tarn Hows has been a hugely popular destination for tourists for well over a century now, but careful management means that it remains a beautiful place to be with delightful views.

This walk starts at the car park at Tarn Hows and finishes with a stroll on its broad paths down its full length. The green, tree-covered shores make a fine contrast with Holme Fell, a rugged and wild top that Wainwright calls 'one of the most attractive of Lakeland's fells.' The way up it begins at Yew Tree Farm, also once owned by Beatrix Potter and now by the National Trust, and one of the most photographed buildings in the Lake District, especially since it doubled as Hill Top in the film story of Potter's life starring Renée Zellweger. The route up is easy enough for most children, and the summit area is a rocky platform that is ideal for exploring and picnics. Because the top is fairly isolated and exposed, the panoramic views are terrific, taking in most of Coniston Water and the Coniston fells.

This area also bears the scars of slate mining, once a major industry in the Lake District. On the way back down to Tarn Hows from Holme Fell you will see old quarries and tarns that were built as reservoirs to serve the miners, while further on at Hodge Close are some enormous mine openings. They are now long abandoned, but the cliffs and rocks that were left behind are now very popular among climbers, who you may see clinging precariously to the sides, while their murky interiors are often used by cave divers and explorers. Holme Fell and Tarn Hows are not quite so dramatic as that, but they do make for a very good morning or afternoon worth of walking for families.

From *Book Four: The Southern Fells*

Distance 4½ miles (7.2km)

Ascent 800 feet (245m)

Start and finish point The pay-and-display National Trust car park at Tarn Hows (SD 327 996). It is free to National Trust members

Ordnance Survey maps Explorer OL7; Landranger 90 and 96

Getting there

Tarn Hows is in the middle of a triangle between Coniston, Hawkshead and Skelwith Bridge near Ambleside. It is well signposted from surrounding roads.

From Coniston, head towards Hawkshead and turn off to the left at Monk Coniston. From Hawkshead and Skelwith Bridge, head towards Hakwshead Hill and look for the turn-off on the right. The car park can fill up quickly on summer days, though turnover is quite fast so you may not have to wait long for a space.

Public transport access to the start of the walk is limited to the X30 or Tarn Hows Tourer bus, which links it to Coniston and Hawkshead, though it is restricted to several services a day and is periodically threatened, so check on Cumbria's Traveline (0871 200 2233, www.traveline.info) before depending on it. Monk Coniston, less than a mile from the starting point, can be reached on the 505 bus, which runs to stops including Coniston, Hawkshead, Far Sawrey and Ambleside. Ask the driver for the

Monk Coniston stop, and then take the road up towards Tarn Hows, looking out for the turn-off path to the left indicated in the directions, signposted for Lew Yewdale.

Facilities, food and drink
The car park at Tarn Hows has toilets, and hosts an ice cream van during the summer.

The nearest places for food and drink are in Coniston and Hawkshead, both of which have plenty of options, and Skelwith Bridge. The Outgate Inn (015394 36413, www.outgateinn.co.uk) and the more food-oriented Drunken Duck Inn at Barngates (015394 36347, www.drunkenduckinn.co.uk) are both recommended between Hawkshead and Ambleside, as is the Chesters café at Skelwith Bridge (015394 34711, www.chestersbytheriver.co.uk).

Yew Tree Farm, a mile or so into the walk off the A593, is a fine place to stay, and takes bookings for large groups for afternoon tea, though it no longer caters for drop-in visitors (015394 41433, www.yewtree-farm.com).

Directions
1 Leave the car park and turn left on to the road, following it as it bends downhill. After nearly ½ mile (800m), at a junction take a footpath on your right, signposted for Low Yewdale, and pass through a wooden gate. The track becomes a smoother road and drops down to Tarn Hows cottage. Just in front of the house turn right, and soon pass through a gate. Here turn left and follow the fence for a few steps before bending off half right and descending to pass through a gate in the fence. The path becomes clearer as you descend further, eventually reaching the main road (SD 320 998).

2 Turn right along the road for a few paces, and then cross it carefully to enter the drive to Yew Tree Farm. A few steps up the drive, leave it on the footpath signposted for Coniston; it seems like the wrong direction, but it is not. Soon the track

meets a side path to the right by a wall corner. Take this path, which wends through bracken and a wooden gate, and bends right to enter Harry Guards Wood. Where the path splits, indicated by two footpath arrows, take the left-hand fork to start the slog up Holme Fell. It leads you to a col between two higher points called Uskdale Gap. Turn left here for the short diversion up to the cairn (NY 315 007). As Wainwright notes, there are two subsidiary cairns near by, but this one will do for most walkers.

3 Back at Uskdale Gap, continue on the main path, which descends with a disused reservoir on your left and a disused quarry on your right. The path reaches a T-junction by a wall; here turn right, soon passing through a large wooden gate. Ignore the next wooden gate off to your left, which leads to more and much larger disused quarries, and instead follow the path to the right, with a fence on your left-hand side. When you reach the next gate, turn right, the way signposted for High Oxenfell. The path leads to a farm, where it becomes a narrow road. Continue along it to a fork, where you continue ahead, signposted for the A593. It leads you down to the main road (NY 328 018).

4 Carefully cross the road and take the narrow road immediately opposite, signposted for High Arnside Farm. Where the road bends left, leave it on a rough track to the right, signposted for the public footpath to Tarn Hows. After about ½ mile (800m) it reaches another junction, where you leave the track to the right through a small gate, signposted for Tarn Hows and Coniston. After ¼ mile (400m) more, Tarn Hows comes into sight.

5 At the path junction with the tarn in view, turn right, signposted for Coniston and the car park. The delightful path now leads for nearly a mile around the western side of the tarn to its southern corner. After passing through a gate, take the middle path of three that face you. It winds up to the car park.

Holme Fell

from Tunnel Quarry
Low Fell

from the north ridge
(Ivy Crag on the left)

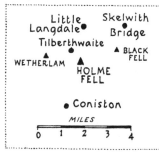

Little
Langdale •
          Skelwith
          Bridge
Tilberthwaite •
                ▲ BLACK
                  FELL
WETHERLAM ▲
          HOLME
          FELL ▲

• Coniston

MILES
0   1   2   3   4

the big cairn of Ivy Crag
(there are uncairned outcrops nearby
at a slightly higher elevation)

134

MAP

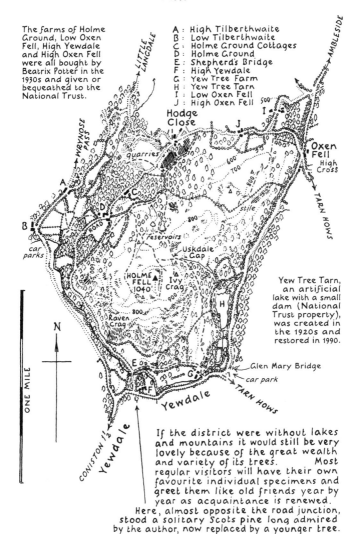

The farms of Holme Ground, Low Oxen Fell, High Yewdale and High Oxen Fell were all bought by Beatrix Potter in the 1930s and given or bequeathed to the National Trust.

A : High Tilberthwaite
B : Low Tilberthwaite
C : Holme Ground Cottages
D : Holme Ground
E : Shepherd's Bridge
F : High Yewdale
G : Yew Tree Farm
H : Yew Tree Tarn
I : Low Oxen Fell
J : High Oxen Fell

LITTLE LANGDALE

AMBLESIDE

WRYNOSE PASS

Hodge Close

Oxen Fell High Cross

quarries

TARN HOWS

car parks

stile

reservoirs

Uskdale Cap

HOLME FELL 1040

Ivy Crag

Raven Crag

H

Yew Tree Tarn, an artificial lake with a small dam (National Trust property), was created in the 1920s and restored in 1990.

N

ONE MILE

E

G

F

Glen Mary Bridge

car park

TARN HOWS

Yewdale

CONISTON 1½

Yewdale

If the district were without lakes and mountains it would still be very lovely because of the great wealth and variety of its trees. Most regular visitors will have their own favourite individual specimens and greet them like old friends year by year as acquaintance is renewed. Here, almost opposite the road junction, stood a solitary Scots pine long admired by the author, now replaced by a younger tree.

NATURAL FEATURES

It is a characteristic of many of Lakeland's lesser heights that what they lack in elevation they make up in ruggedness. Slopes a thousand feet high can be just as steep and rough as those three times as long, while crags occur at all levels and are by no means the preserve of the highest peaks, so that the climbing of a small hill, what there is of it, can call for as much effort, over a shorter time, as a big one; moreover, the lower tops have the further defence of a tangle of tough vegetation, usually heather and bracken, through which progress is a far more laborious task than on the grassy slopes of higher zones. Such a one is Holme Fell, at the head of Yewdale, isolated by valleys yet very much under the dominance of Wetherlam. A craggy southern front, a switchback ridge, a couple of small but very beautiful tree-girt tarns (old reservoirs), and a great quarry that reveals the core of colourful slate lying beneath the glorious jungle of juniper and birch, heather and bracken, make this one of the most attractive of Lakeland's fells.

ASCENTS

The worst roughnesses may be avoided, fortunately, by using a charming path that crosses the fell north of the summit. From the east, the path starts at Yew Tree Farm and slants upwards, mostly amongst trees, to Uskdale Gap on the ridge, where the cairn on Ivy Crag is in sight and quickly reached. From the west, the path may be joined above Holme Ground (see map), in which case it is not necessary to continue quite as far as the Gap, the main summit being gained by a scramble on the right.

THE SUMMIT

The highest point is a platform of naked rock, set at the top of slabs, in the middle of a summit-ridge with a continuous escarpment on the east side. 200 yards away, across a heathery plateau, is the subsidiary summit of Ivy Crag, identified by a big cairn.

DESCENTS: Uskdale Gap is the key to easy descent. Avoid the steep southern declivities, which are much too rough for comfort.

THE VIEW

Outstanding in a moderate view is the striking full length of Coniston Water; this is the best place for viewing the lake.

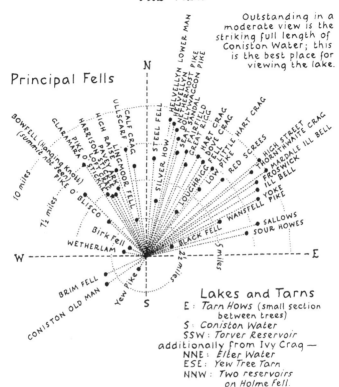

Principal Fells

(The diagram shows directional sight-lines to fells, labelled:)

N, S, E, W

BOWFELL (Hanging Knott) (summit not seen), GLARAMARA, PIKE O' STICKLE, HARRISON STICKLE, PAVEY ARK, HIGH RAISE, LINGMOOR FELL, CALF CRAG, ULLSCARF, STEEL FELL, SILVER HOW, HELVELLYN LOWER MAN, HELVELLYN, NETHERMOST PIKE, DOLLYWAGGON PIKE, FAIRFIELD, SEAT SANDAL, GREAT RIGG, HART CRAG, DOVE CRAG, HART CRAG, LITTLE HART CRAG, LOUGHRIGG FELL, LOW PIKE, RED SCREES, HIGH STREET, THORNTHWAITE CRAG, MARDALE ILL BELL, FROSWICK, ILL BELL, YOKE, WANSFELL PIKE, SALLOWS, SOUR HOWES, BLACK FELL, BIRK FELL, WETHERLAM, BRIM FELL, CONISTON OLD MAN, YEW PIKE

10 miles, 7½ miles, 5 miles, 2½ miles

Lakes and Tarns

E: *Tarn Hows (small section between trees)*
S: *Coniston Water*
SSW: *Torver Reservoir*
additionally from Ivy Crag —
NNE: *Elter Water*
ESE: *Yew Tree Tarn*
NNW: *Two reservoirs on Holme Fell.*

The Hodge Close quarries are still used for the extraction of stone. The travelling crane and mineral railway have gone, but there is still an emerald lake, and the two tremendous holes are very impressive. The disused northern quarry may be entered by a steep path at the northern end and its stony floor crossed to the arch connecting with the second quarry and the green lake. Much of the quarry waste has been colonised by birches.

The arch

12 Claife Heights
from Far Sawrey

Most Lake District fell walks have a distinct peak to aim for, but the summit of Claife Heights is not really the purpose of this walk. Instead it is the dense forest that provides the main attraction, making for a refreshing change from the rugged fellside scenery that characterises most Lake District climbs.

This walk starts in the small village of Far Sawrey, and winds pleasantly up to Claife Heights via tarns including Moss Eccles Tarn, man-made but still one of the prettiest of the many to be seen in the Lake District and a fine place for a rest or picnic. The way up through the forest itself is on clear and well-signed paths and is mostly easy underfoot, though there is a short scramble over a felled area and there may be diversions in place because of other forestry work. The summit is sheltered by trees and so doesn't offer many views – in fact, if it didn't have an Ordnance Survey trig point on top it would be easily missed – but is still a nice spot to rest.

Claife Heights was nevertheless a popular viewing point for early tourists to the Lakes in the nineteenth century, who would climb up to Claife Station at the southern end of the forest to inspect the surroundings through coloured glass windows, intended to enhance the effects of the changing seasons on the fells and lake. The Station, built in the 1790s, is now in ruins but still accessible.

Families will enjoy this walk's close associations with Beatrix Potter, one of the Lake District's many famous authors and now perhaps its biggest export. She set many of her stories in Far Sawrey and the countryside around, and walked often on Claife Heights, from which she drew much of her inspiration. She also rowed with her husband on Moss Eccles Tarn, which may well have inspired her tale of Jeremy Fisher. Potter later bought the tarn with the royalties from her books, and bequeathed it to the National Trust, along with her house and large swathes of properties and land around the Lake District.

From *The Outlying Fells of Lakeland*

Distance 5 miles (8km)

Ascent 500 feet (150m)

Start and finish point The car park by Braithwaite Hall in Far Sawrey (SD 379 954). There are honesty boxes for the £2 a day parking fee

Ordnance Survey maps Explorer OL7; Landranger 96

Getting there

Far Sawrey is on the B5285, about 3 miles (4.8km) from Hawkshead via an attractive drive along the shores of Esthwaite Water. But many people prefer to reach the village via the ferry over Windermere from Bowness, which carries cars as well as pedestrians and deposits you by the Ferry House on the western side. As well as being a useful shortcut across Windermere, the ferry is a nice way to see the lake and Claife Heights up ahead. It runs every 20 minutes from around 7am on weekdays (9am on Sundays, and nearer 10am in winter), and you can sometimes wait a while in summer as it carries only eighteen cars at a time. It will not run at all in very bad weather; look out for roadside notices about its status or call 01228 227653 if in doubt.

From the Ferry House it is about a mile up the B5285 to the start of this walk in Far Sawrey, and those on foot can shorten it slightly with a footpath near the end. The walk described here can conclude at the ferry – follow the diversion in the directions below – so it is a very good one to do from Bowness without a car.

From early April to late October, a minibus service (number 525) connects Ferry House with Hawkshead via Far Sawrey about ten times a day, so saving the mile's walk up to the start. Hakwshead is in turn connected to Ambleside and Coniston by the 505 bus.

Facilities, food and drink

The Cuckoo Brow Inn in Far Sawrey, a few steps from the start of the walk, welcomes children, dogs and muddy boots, and serves good sandwiches and fuller meals (015394 43425, www.cuckoobrow.co.uk). Formerly called the Sawrey Hotel, it is also a nice place to stay.

Given this area's close ties to Beatrix Potter, children may well like to combine the walk with a visit to Hill Top in Near Sawrey, where she lived and wrote (015394 36269, www.nationaltrust.org.uk/hilltop). It is maintained by the National Trust just as it was when Potter lived there, and has a pretty cottage garden and shop. The house is open from mid-February to the end of October, but can get very busy in the summer when you might have to wait to enter on a timed ticket. The 525 bus can take you there from Far Sawrey or the Ferry House. Near Sawrey also has The Tower Bank Arms, a picture-postcard pub that is featured in Potter's stories and is very child and pet-friendly (015394 36334, www.towerbankarms.co.uk), and a playground. The nearest shops are in Hawkshead or back across the ferry in Bowness.

Directions

1 Turn left out of the car park, towards and past the Cuckoo Brow Inn. Take the first turn on your right after the inn, marked by a blue sign for Cuckoo Brow Lane. About 110 yards (100m) after the road crosses a cattle grid, leave it on a path to the left, indicated by a blue public bridleway arrow. Soon cross a stream via a little wooden footbridge, and continue up to a wooden gate. Pass through and continue up to another wooden gate. Pass through and continue ahead through a metal gate. This rough track now climbs gently, via another wooden gate, to the eastern shores of the lovely Moss Eccles Tarn (SD 373 968).

2 Continue along the very clear track, and after about ½ mile (800m) pass between two more tarns: a large one, Wise Een

Tarn, on your left, and a smaller one on your right. The track now rises up grassier slopes to enter the Claife forest through a wooden gate and becomes a broader forest track. Where it descends and turns left on a hairpin bend, leave it to the right, on a path signposted for Ferry and Far Sawrey (SD 377 982). The path is now less distinct, rising up across a felled area of the forest and then climbing ahead, further into the forest proper. It winds along to a large stone viewpoint (SD 380 979) and then descends to a broad forest track.

3 Turn right on to the track (signposted for Ferry and Far Sawrey), but leave it about 75 yards (70m) later on a footpath to the left, again signposted for Far Sawrey and Ferry. After 165 yards (150m), turn right at a junction of paths. After 100m of climbing, turn left at a signpost marked Viewpoint, and walk up to the Ordnance Survey column, on the top of the second rocky outcrop that you pass (SD 382 973). This is the summit, called High Blind How, though the views are mostly obscured by trees.

4 Drop back down to the Viewpoint sign, and turn left. The path now descends through the forest, with occasional signposts for Ferry. Look out for forestry signs too, and obey any diversions that may be in place because of felling operations. Further down, the path picks up a wall on your left and then a fence to your right, and eventually reaches a gate. Pass through, and continue on the clear track ahead, again with a wall or fence on your left, to another gate.

5 Continue on, with the wall still alongside you, to a crossroads of paths and a signpost (SD 382 959). Here you can turn left for the ferry over the lake to Bowness, but for Far Sawrey turn right. The path leads to another gate, this time with a wall on your right, then on down into the village, with the car park directly over the road where you emerge.

Claife Heights
886'
500 feet of ascent

from *FAR SAWREY*
5 miles
3 hours

from Esthwaite Water

Claife Heights is the naturally-wooded and man-afforested upland rising between Esthwaite Water and Windermere. It has not a well-defined summit, the highest point (886 feet, north of Pate Crags) having an Ordnance Survey column now surrounded by conifers but accessible by a path. In this upland Beatrix Potter loved to wander. Its best feature is a series of tarns in lovely settings: reservoirs actually but not obtrusively artificial; none of them appears on 19th century maps. The most attractive of these is Moss Eccles Tarn, which has a glimpse of Windermere and is a charming spot for a siesta. Wise Een Tarn is more open and has a view to the Langdales. Three Dubs Tarn is deeply inurned in a surround of tall trees, but inaccessible: it has a boat-house, better built than most.

Claife Heights is delightful. It was more so before forestry curtailed walking and restricted the views.

Moss Eccles Tarn

Wise Een Tarn

It matters little whether the walk is commenced at Near or Far Sawrey but as the finish is at the latter village it is more convenient to make it the starting point. There is a car park opposite the telephone kiosk.

Take the tarmac lane rising on the west side of the Sawrey Hotel, leaving it by a path forking left beyond a cattle grid. Cross a stream (watercress here) and enter a lane to join a rough road coming up from Near Sawrey. Follow this to a gate below Moss Eccles Tarn, whence it continues over open ground as a cart-track and, skirting Wise Een Tarn, becomes a less distinct footpath rising into the forest ahead, where it assumes the dimensions of a forest road. Stay on the road where it bends right, but turn right where it bends left at a signpost. The path is not easy to follow. At the next signpost (bearing the number 7) turn right onto a clearer path. At first the path heads southwest beside a broken wall. Then it turns through 180° and heads northeast. Finally it curves round to the right and reveals, unexpectedly, an open view on the left of the Ambleside district. When you come to a forest road turn right, and then left at a white-topped signpost opposite a tarn. In 150 yards turn right, and then left at a signpost saying 'Viewpoint'. This path leads to the Ordnance Survey column. A small area around the column has been left unplanted, and there are glimpses of the view, but most of it is hidden by trees.

Return to the main path and turn left. At the next two signposts take the path to the ferry, and at the signpost numbered 4 the old path from Belle Grange to Sawrey is joined. Turn right here. The path becomes a cart-track and leads back into Far Sawrey (a branch going off to the Windermere Ferry) by the lane coming down on the east side of the hotel.

Far Sawrey is so called because it is farther from Hawkshead than Near Sawrey, which is famous as the home of Beatrix Potter and the setting for many of her illustrations.

*Three Dubs Tarn
(on private ground)*

144

MAP

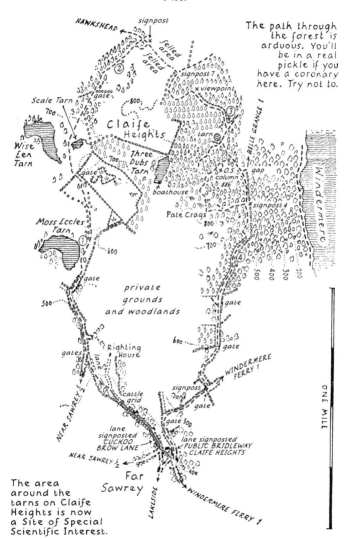

HAWKSHEAD ← signpost

The path through the forest is arduous. You'll be in a real pickle if you have a coronary here. Try not to.

Felled area
Felled area
signpost 7
× viewpoint
③

Scale Tarn
gate
800
700
Claife Heights
tarn
BELLE GRANGE 1

Wise Een Tarn
Three Dubs Tarn
700
gap
Windermere

gate
boathouse
× O.S. column 886
signpost 4

Moss Eccles Tarn
Pate Crags
700
800

①
600
gate
600

gate
private grounds and woodlands
gate
600

500
gate
400 300 200

Righting House
lane
gates
gate
WINDERMERE FERRY 1

cattle grid
signpost
gate

NEAR SAWREY ½
lane signposted CUCKOO BROW LANE
gate 300
lane signposted PUBLIC BRIDLEWAY CLAIFE HEIGHTS

NEAR SAWREY ½
400

Far Sawrey
LAKESIDE
WINDERMERE FERRY 1

ONE MILE

The area around the tarns on Claife Heights is now a Site of Special Scientific Interest.

13 Nab Scar
from Rydal

It is Nab Scar's proximity to Rydal, and that village's close ties with William Wordsworth and his fellow Romantic poets, that has brought the fell to many people's attention over the years. Wordsworth and his contemporaries were enthusiastic fell walkers as well as writers, and would have strode out on to Nab Scar from his home at Rydal Mount at the foot of the fell.

It is also known as the first summit on the Fairfield horseshoe, one of the best long ridge walks in the Lake District. This walk provides a fine taster of the horseshoe, and brings the length of the popular circuit into view. The next stop on the horseshoe is Heron Pike, which like Nab Scar is described by Wainwright in *The Eastern Fells*, and which can be easily added to the walk by anyone wanting to add it to their collection of peaks by extending things slightly at the point suggested in the directions. But there is not much to be seen from there that cannot be enjoyed from Nab Scar, which has good views of many lakes and tarns as well as the Coniston fells and the Langdale Pikes.

For those happy enough to have reached Nab Scar, the walk descends on its western side to take in Alcock Tarn, an attractive tarn named after the nineteenth-century landowner who enlarged it so he could stock it with trout for fishing. After dropping down by Grasmere, it returns to Rydal via the cheerily named Coffin Route – the path that was built to take the deceased from Rydal and Ambleside, in times when those places did not have burial grounds, to the churchyard in Grasmere. Wordsworth would have walked this way many times, either from Rydal Mount or his previous home of Dove Cottage in Grasmere.

The path along the Coffin Route provides 1½ mile (2.4km) of very easy walking, and the way up to Nab Scar from Rydal is also straightforward, though a steady slog. One of the pleasures of ridge walks like the Fairfield horseshoe is that the route and target fells are obvious up ahead, and this is true on the way from Rydal. Parents coaxing their children up Nab Scar from there can gaze along the ridge and look forward to the day when they will be able to manage the whole horseshoe.

From *Book One: The Eastern Fells*

Distance 4½ miles (7.2km)

Ascent 1,200 feet (365m)

Start and finish point The free car parking spaces on the road up to Rydal Hall and Rydal Mount (NY 365 062)

Ordnance Survey maps Explorer OL7; Landranger 90

Getting there
Except on the busiest summer days, there is usually parking to be had on the road up to Rydal Hall and Rydal Mount. It is just off the A591 between Ambleside and Grasmere; look out for the signposts, on the right as you drive from Ambleside. Leave a donation for the church in the honesty boxes in the wall. If the roadside spaces are full up, there is more parking a little way back towards Ambleside at Pelter Bridge (NY 366 059), or further away towards Grasmere at the White Moss car park (NY 348 066). Use the footpath back to Rydal to avoid the A592 if you use the second of these, and divert to it on the way back to Rydal.

The 555 bus, running between the north of the Lake District at Keswick and the south at Kendal, stops right by the junction at Rydal for the church, Hall and Mount, from where it is a steep walk up to the start of the walk. To link the walk up to trains, head for Windermere on the Lakes Line and catch the 555 bus towards Keswick from the station.

Facilities, food and drink

Rydal has plenty of options for walkers wanting food and drink and more places to explore. Rydal Mount, Wordsworth's home for nearly 40 years until his death in 1850, has tours of the house and gardens plus a tearoom (015394 33002, www.rydalmount.co.uk). Rydal Hall was a family home for centuries but was sold to the Carlisle Diocese in the 1960s and is now a Christian centre (015394 32050, www.rydalhall.org). Its gardens are open for everyone to explore, and it has an excellent tearoom in the old school house, open daily all year round.

At the bottom of the hill down from Rydal Mount and Hall, St Mary's Church is worth a visit. Wordsworth was a church warden here and, after the death of his daughter in 1847, renamed a patch of land he had bought near by as Dora's Field; its daffodils and bluebells make a spectacular site in spring. Turning right a short way from Rydal's junction brings you to the Badger Bar, part of the Glen Rothay Hotel, which serves decent bar meals (015394 34500, www.theglenrothay.co.uk). There are many more eating options and tourist attractions in Ambleside and Grasmere, both close by on the A591.

Directions

1 Walk up the steep road from wherever you have managed to park along it. At the top, by Rydal Mount, continue up with the house on your left, and a few steps later, at a fork with the Coffin Route to Grasmere on your left (the way on which you will return later) continue ahead again to pass some houses. Leave the road where it runs out to take a footpath on your right, passing through a wooden gate after a few steps.

2 The path up to Nab Scar is now very clear, winding steeply over stone slabs at first and then becoming rougher. Don't forget to look back for wonderful panoramas and, nearer the top, to turn left for vertiginous views over Rydal Water. Towards the top of Nab Scar the path flattens, and the actual summit is marked by a nicely built cairn to the left of the path, soon after crossing a dry stone wall (NY 355 072).

3 The path along the ridge on towards Lord's Crag and Heron Pike is similarly clear. It is marked by the remains of a dry stone wall, and then by occasional cairns. Continue on to Heron Pike if you want to add the peak to your collection, the summit marked by a rocky outcrop (NY 356 083). Otherwise, leave the ridge route by one of the cairns a few hundred metres before Heron Pike (NY 355 080), picking up a grassy path. Within 45 yards (40m) you should see Alcock Tarn below you. Descend to the tarn. The path is indistinct for a while, and care is needed on the grassy slopes, especially in the wet, but the tarn remains in front of you to guide your way, and further down the way through the bracken is clearer. You arrive at the tarn through a gap in a dry stone wall.

4 Follow the path to the left of the tarn, and leave it at its far corner on a path that takes you through a gap in a wall. The path continues with a rocky outcrop to your left, with the village of Grasmere and Rydal Water soon opening up in front of you. This very pleasant path descends steadily, reaching a junction of footpaths just ahead of an enclosed wood. Here turn left. The path descends further, passing through two metal gates, and reaches a T-junction with a road (NY 345 068).

5 Turn left here, the way signposted as the Coffin Route to Rydal. The path passes White Moss Tarn to your left, and soon becomes a track, but the way back to Rydal is very clear for 1½ miles (2.4km). It emerges on the steep road where the walk started; turn right for the car parking spaces.

Nab Scar

1450'

- ▲ FAIRFIELD
- ▲ GREAT RIGG
- ▲ STONE ARTHUR
- ▲ HERON PIKE
- • Grasmere ▲ NAB SCAR
- • Rydal
- Ambleside •

MILES
0 1 2 3 4

from Rydal Water

NATURAL FEATURES

Nab Scar is well known. Its associations with the Lake Poets who came to dwell at the foot of its steep wooded slopes have invested it with romance, and its commanding position overlooking Rydal Water brings it to the notice of the many visitors to that charming lake. It is a fine abrupt height, with a rough, craggy south face; on the flanks are easier slopes. Elevated ground continues beyond the summit and rises gently to Heron Pike. Nab Scar is not a separate fell, but is merely the butt of the long southern ridge of Fairfield.

MAP

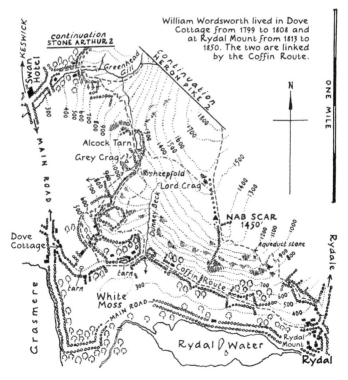

William Wordsworth lived in Dove Cottage from 1799 to 1808 and at Rydal Mount from 1813 to 1850. The two are linked by the Coffin Route.

ASCENTS

The popular ascent is from Rydal, a charming climb along a good path, steep in its middle reaches; this is the beginning of the 'Fairfield Horseshoe' when it is walked clockwise. Nab Scar can also be reached from the Swan Hotel by means of a path that rises from the south end of Alcock Tarn.

THE SUMMIT

Strictly, Nab Scar is the name of the craggy south face, not of the fell rising above it, but its recognised summit is a tall edifice of stones built well back from the edge of the cliffs, near a crumbled wall that runs north towards Heron Pike. Hereabouts the immediate surroundings are uninteresting, the redeeming feature being the fine view.

Nab Scar has a subterranean watercourse: below its surface the Thirlmere aqueduct runs through a tunnel. The scars of this operation are nearly gone, but evidence of the existence of the tunnel remains alongside the Rydal path, above the steepest part: here may be found a block of stone a yard square set in the ground; it bears no inscription but marks the position of the tunnel directly beneath.

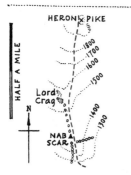

RIDGE ROUTE

To HERON PIKE, 2008': ⅔ mile: N
570 feet of ascent
An easy climb on grass
A plain path accompanies the old wall, then it keeps to the right of the ridge.

THE VIEW

This is an 'unbalanced' view, most of it being exceptionally dull, the rest exceptionally charming. Lakes and tarns are a very special feature of the delightful prospect to south and west and the grouping of the Coniston and Langdale fells is quite attractive.

Principal Fells

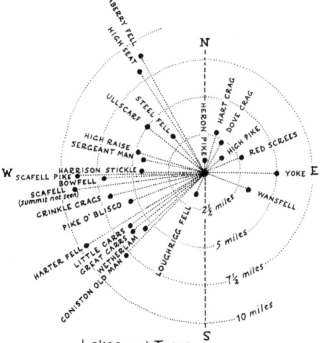

Lakes and Tarns

SSE : Windermere
S : Blelham Tarn
S : Esthwaite Water
SSW : Coniston Water
SW : Elterwater
WSW : Grasmere
WNW : Easedale Tarn
NW : Alcock Tarn

14 Wansfell
from Ambleside

This walk combines the summit of Wansfell, part of the ridge of Caudale Moor, with the Stock Ghyll waterfalls, a popular sight for tourists to Ambleside ever since they first started arriving here in Victorian times.

The waterfalls are a short but sharp pull up from the town centre, and the path to the top of them might be a walk enough for small children, who can observe them from safe viewpoints. The succession of falls once powered several nearby watermills and the top one drops around 70 feet.

Ambleside's 'local' fell of Wansfell makes a fine continuation on from Stock Ghyll, and has become a very popular climb – so popular, in fact, that the path has had to be rescued from substantial erosion, and replaced for much of the distance by a long succession of stone steps set into the slopes. Flights like this are not very popular among those who prefer their fells to be as rugged as nature intended, but they do make for easy walking for children – though it is nevertheless a steady slog up to the top.

The full distance to the top of Wansfell, on a straight there-and-back route from Ambleside via the waterfalls, is about 5 miles (8km), but it can be shortened by 2 miles (3.2km) by omitting Wansfell itself and making Wansfell Pike the ultimate goal. You do not miss out on much in terms of elevation, and even less in views and walking – though completists will want to reach the fell top proper. To extend the walk, and save on coming back the same way, you could continue on from Wansfell Pike to Troutbeck where indicated in the directions.

From *Book Two: The Far Eastern Fells*

Distance 5 miles (8km)

Ascent 1,500 feet (455m)

Start and finish point The main pay-and-display car park on Rydal Road in Ambleside (NY 376 047)

Ordnance Survey maps Explorer OL7; Landranger 90

Getting there

The car park is off the A591 on the northern side of Ambleside, on the road out of town towards Rydal and Grasmere. There are several other pay-and-display car parks in the town if this one is full. Note that street parking in Ambleside is limited to an hour with a disc, obtainable for free from local shops, and is tightly enforced.

Ambleside is well served by buses. The 555 calls on its long run from Kendal in the south to Keswick in the north. The 505 runs to Coniston and Hawkshead; the 516 to Skelwith Bridge, Elterwater, Chapel Stile and the Old Dungeon Ghyll in the Langdale valley; and the 618 to Newby Bridge and Barrow-in-Furness. The 599 shuttle links Ambleside to Bowness and Windermere and, like the 555, stops at Windermere station for train travelers. All buses stop at Kelsick Road; from here, walk up past the library to the T-junction, turn left, and look for the turning off to the waterfalls in the directions. You can also reach Ambleside via ferry from Bowness or Lakeside over Windermere (015394 43360, www.windermere-lakecruises.co.uk).

If you extend the walk to Troutbeck as indicated in the directions, you can return to Ambleside via Robin Lane and Skelghyll Woods, or find an obliging driver to pick you up from there.

Facilities, food and drink

The car park on Rydal Road has public toilets, and is very convenient for the facilities in Ambleside. You do not have to walk far to find places to eat and drink, and there are several cafés and shops from which to make up a picnic for Wansfell. Particularly recommended places to eat include Sheila's Cottage restaurant and tearooms on the Slack (015394 33079, www.sheilascottage. co.uk); the Apple Pie Café and Bakery close to the car park on Rydal Road (015394 33679, www.theapplepieambleside.co.uk)

and Zeffirelli's on Compston Road, which offers an all-day café and vegetarian restaurant as well as a cinema with several screens (015394 33845, www.zeffirellis.com). Ambleside's best pub is The Golden Rule on Smithy Brow; children are welcome, though not in the bar (015394 32257, www.goldenrule-ambleside.co.uk).

Other family-friendly places include the recreation ground off Compston Road and a large indoor play area off Rothay Road on the west of town (015394 39906, www.ruftytuftys.co.uk). Ambleside also has lots of events, and it is worth trying to get along in particular to the Ambleside or Grasmere Sports, held on the last Thursday in July and last Sunday in August respectively (www.amblesidesports.co.uk and www.grasmeresports.com). They feature traditional Lakeland sports like fell-running and wrestling, and have plenty for children to see and do.

For more, call in at the tourist information centre on Market Cross, passed on the first stretch of the walk from the car park (0844 225 0544, www.thehubofambleside.co.uk).

Families extending the walk to Troutbeck will find a lovely village shop and post office well stocked with snacks and cakes and selling cups of tea (015394 33302; closed on Sundays). There are two well-positioned seventeenth-century pub-hotels with good food, The Queen's Head (015394 32174, www.queensheadhotel.com) and The Mortal Man (015394 33193, www.themortalman.co.uk), and you might also visit Townend, a yeoman farmer's house looked after by the National Trust (015394 32628; www.nationaltrust.org.uk).

Directions

1 Return to the main road from the car park and turn right into the town centre. Continue past two sets of traffic lights and then past the Salutation Hotel on your left. Where the road bends to the right, cross it and take the narrow road to the left of the Market Hall. This is the well-trodden route up to the waterfalls above Ambleside, and meets up with Stock Ghyll, down to your left. After about 435 yards (400m) on this road, leave it to the left on a clear, broad path that is obligingly signposted 'This way to the waterfalls'.

2 This path leads you, as advertised, up to a succession of waterfalls along a path signed with red arrows and with side paths to the left to get closer to them. At the viewpoint for the highest and most spectacular waterfall (sketched by Wainwright in his notes), by a tree and picnic table, take the path to the right marked 'To revolving gate exit' rather than following the red arrow again. This soon rejoins the road used earlier.

3 Turn left up the road. Soon after passing some university buildings on your right, the road becomes rougher and leads up to a bridge. Immediately before the bridge, take a footpath on your right, signposted for Troutbeck via Wansfell (NY 386 046). Wansfell is now directly ahead, and the path leads first alongside a stream to a wooden gate, and then more steeply up stone steps set in the grassy slopes. After just over ½ mile (800m) of steep climbing the steps run out by a large cairn, and a path diverts left for a short scramble up to the summit of Wansfell Pike (NY 394 042).

4 As Wainwright notes, the 1-mile (1.6km) ridge route on from Wansfell Pike to the 'proper' summit of Wansfell does not have a great deal to recommend it, with more ups and downs over featureless and often boggy ground. To reach it, pass through a black metal gate in the fence a few steps from the summit and turn left along the ridge. The path is very clear, clinging to a wall on your left before slanting away up to the summit of Wansfell, marked by a cairn on a grassy knoll (NY 403 051). Return along the ridge and pass back through the black gate to Wansfell Pike.

5 Drop down to the cairn at the top of the steps climbed earlier. To divert to Troutbeck, turn left to pass through the summit fence again, on to a footpath that leads down on to a track, Nanny Lane, and into Troutbeck; the distance is about 1¼ miles (2km). Otherwise, turn right down the stone slabs, through the two wooden gates and left on to the track. Look out for the path to the waterfalls used earlier, on your right, and follow it down to the road. Turn right back to Ambleside, and right again for the car park.

Wansfell

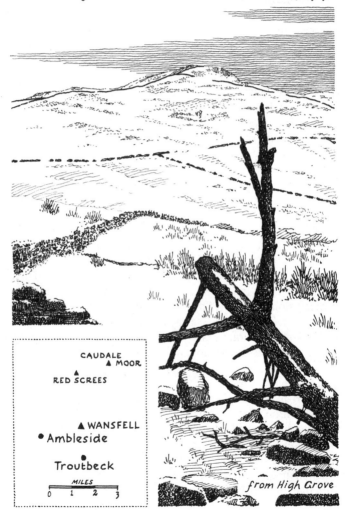

CAUDALE
▲ MOOR
▲
RED SCREES

▲ WANSFELL
● Ambleside
●
Troutbeck

MILES
0 1 2 3

from High Grove

NATURAL FEATURES

Caudale Moor sends out three distinct ridges to the south, and the most westerly and longest of the three descends to a wide depression (crossed by the Kirkstone road) before rising and narrowing along an undulating spur that finally falls to the shores of Windermere. This spur is Wansfell, and, although its summit-ridge is fairly narrow and well-defined, the slopes on most sides are extensive, the fell as a whole occupying a broad tract of territory between Ambleside and the Troutbeck valley. Except northwards, the lower slopes are attractively wooded; the upper reaches are mainly grassy, but at the south-west extremity of the ridge there is a rocky bluff known as Wansfell Pike, which is commonly but incorrectly regarded as the top of the fell. Other crags masked by trees flank the Kirkstone road at Troutbeck, and Jenkins Crag in Skelghyll Wood is a very popular viewpoint. On the eastern flanks of the fell, in the village of Troutbeck, are three wells: St. John's Well, St. James' Well and Margaret's Well. Although no longer used as a source of water they can still be easily identified by their inscriptions.

MAP

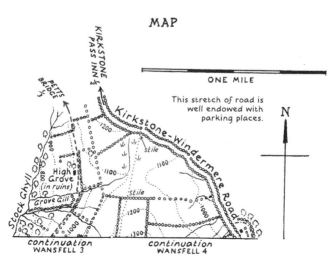

ONE MILE

This stretch of road is well endowed with parking places.

N

continuation WANSFELL 3   continuation WANSFELL 4

MAP

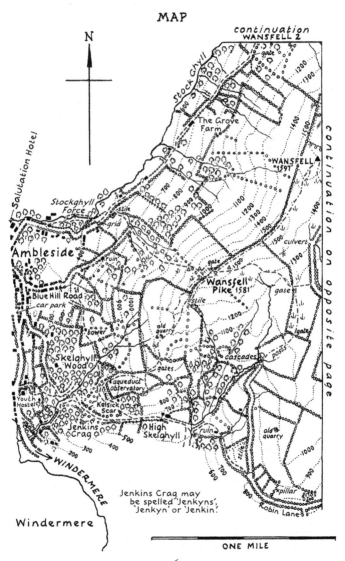

continuation
WANSFELL 2

N

Salutation Hotel

Stockghyll Force

stile

grid

Ambleside

ruin

Blue Hill Road
car park

tower

Skelghyll Wood

aqueduct
observatory

Kelsick Scar

Youth Hostel

Jenkins Crag

High Skelghyll

WINDERMERE

Windermere

Stock Ghyll

gate

The Grove Farm

WANSFELL
1597

gate

Wansfell Pike 1581

stile

old quarry

gates

cascades

culvert

gate

ruin

old quarry

pillar

Robin Lane

continuation on opposite page

Jenkins Crag may
be spelled 'Jenkyns',
'Jenkyn' or 'Jenkin'.

ONE MILE

MAP

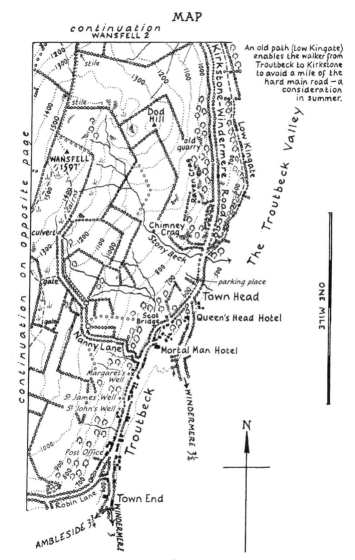

continuation
WANSFELL 2

An old path (Low Kingate) enables the walker from Troutbeck to Kirkstone to avoid a mile of the hard main road — a consideration in summer.

Kirkstone-Windermere Road

Low Kingate

The Troutbeck Valley

1200
1300
stile
1300
1200
1100
1000
Dod Hill
old quarry
Raven Crag
stile
1400
1500
WANSFELL 1597
cairns
1500
1400
1300
Chimney Crag
Stony Beck
800
culvert
1200
1100
1000
700
600
parking place
Town Head
Queen's Head Hotel
gate
1300
gate
Scot Bridges
Mortal Man Hotel
Nanny Lane
Margaret's Well
St James' Well
St John's Well
WINDERMERE 3½
N
1000
Post Office
800
600
500
400
200
100
Robin Lane
Troutbeck
Town End
AMBLESIDE 3¾
WINDERMERE 3

ONE MILE

ASCENT FROM AMBLESIDE
1500 feet of ascent : 2½ miles

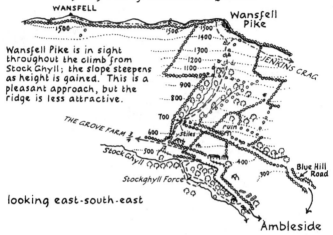

Wansfell Pike is in sight throughout the climb from Stock Ghyll; the slope steepens as height is gained. This is a pleasant approach, but the ridge is less attractive.

looking east-south-east

ASCENT FROM TROUTBECK
1100 feet of ascent : 1¾ miles

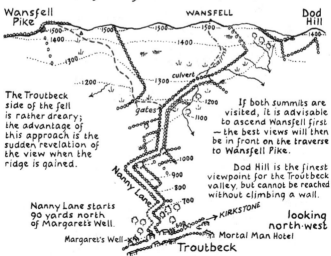

The Troutbeck side of the fell is rather dreary; the advantage of this approach is the sudden revelation of the view when the ridge is gained.

Nanny Lane starts 90 yards north of Margaret's Well.

If both summits are visited, it is advisable to ascend Wansfell first — the best views will then be in front on the traverse to Wansfell Pike.

Dod Hill is the finest viewpoint for the Troutbeck valley, but cannot be reached without climbing a wall.

looking north-west

THE SUMMIT

The recognised summit of Wansfell is marked by a slender tapering cairn about four feet high, but the 2½" map shows a spot height farther north, beyond the fence and broken wall, which suggests that this is the highest point. A mile to the south-west is the lower summit of Wansfell Pike, where there is a step-stile from which paths go down to Ambleside (west) and Troutbeck (east).

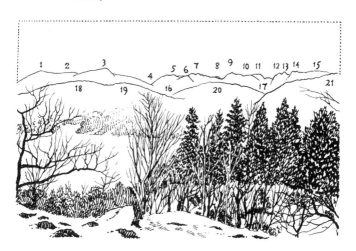

The view westwards from Jenkins Crag

1 : Coniston Old Man
2 : Brim Fell
3 : Wetherlam
4 : Wrynose Pass
5 : Cold Pike
6 : Pike o'Blisco
7 : Crinkle Crags
8 : Scafell
9 : Bowfell
10 : Esk Pike
11 : Great End
12 : Loft Crag
13 : Pike o'Stickle
14 : Harrison Stickle
15 : Pavey Ark
16 : Little Langdale
17 : Great Langdale
18 : Black Fell
19 : Park Fell
20 : Lingmoor Fell
21 : Loughrigg Fell

THE VIEW
FROM THE SUMMIT OF WANSFELL

As a viewpoint, the highest part of the summit is inferior to the lower Wansfell Pike, and, curiously, fewer fells can be seen. Nevertheless, the prospect westwards is very charming.

Principal Fells

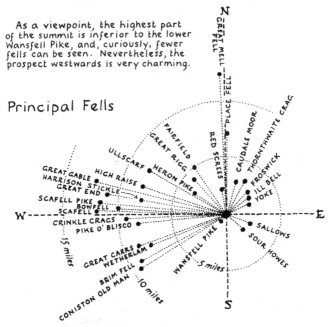

Lakes and Tarns

S : Windermere
WSW : Little Langdale Tarn
W : Grasmere
W : Rydal Water

Red Screes, from the summit

164

THE VIEW
FROM WANSFELL PIKE

Wansfell Pike excels in its view of Windermere, the graceful curve of the lake showing to great advantage. Westwards, the scene is especially beautiful.
Red Screes is a fine object in the north; the east is dull.

Principal Fells

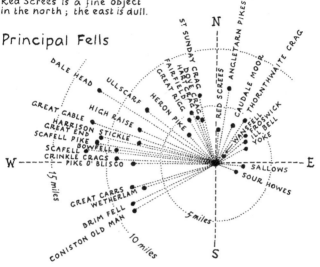

Lakes and Tarns

S : Windermere
SW : Blelham Tarn
W : Little Langdale Tarn
WNW : Grasmere
WNW : Rydal Water
The two sheets of water on the lower slopes of Sour Howes, southeast, are reservoirs.

Windermere, from Wansfell Pike

165

RIDGE ROUTE

To CAUDALE MOOR, 2502'
4½ miles: N, then NE and E
Depression at 1100'
1550 feet of ascent

A long, easy, uninteresting trudge.

In May 2005, when the Countryside and Rights of Way Act came into effect, this route benefited from the removal of PRIVATE notices and the provision of stiles between Wansfell and the main road. A stile has since appeared in the wall at 1700'. The route is on grass all the way. It is safe in mist, but marshy patches will then prove unpleasant.

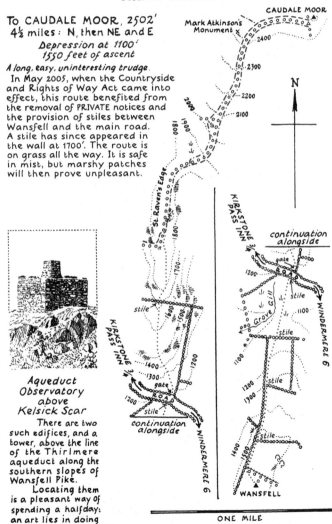

Aqueduct Observatory above Kelsick Scar

There are two such edifices, and a tower, above the line of the Thirlmere aqueduct along the southern slopes of Wansfell Pike.

Locating them is a pleasant way of spending a half day: an art lies in doing this *sans* wallscaling.

CAUDALE MOOR

Mark Atkinson's Monument ×

2400

2300

2200

2100

N

St. Raven's Edge

2000

1900

1800

1700

1600

1500

stile

1400

1300

gate

1200

stile

continuation alongside

KIRKSTONE PASS INN ¾

KIRKSTONE PASS INN ¾

WINDERMERE 6

continuation alongside

1200

gate

stile

1200

1300

1400

Grove Grill

1100

1100

stile

1100

1200

1300

stile

1400

1500

stile

WANSFELL

WINDERMERE 6

ONE MILE

Stockghyll Force

15 Black Combe
from Whicham

Most of the walks in this book are circular, but this one is a straightforward up-and-down on an entirely clear path, and about as simple as navigation gets in the Lake District.

That is not to say it is an entirely easy walk, as the climbing is steady and continuous almost from the very start. But the broad, dry and easy paths make it ideal for children, who can safely run ahead and lead the way to the top. It is also notable for being just about the westernmost of all Lakeland peaks and, as a result, almost as close as you can get on the fells to the aspect of the Lake District that is often overlooked – its coast. The wild and largely deserted Cumbrian coastline can be looked down on during this walk, and it will often be within sound as well as sight.

As Wainwright points out in his notes, Black Combe is an unmistakeable fell, visible from miles around and rising grandly from the sea, 'overtopping all else like a huge whale stranded on a beach'. Its isolation makes it a terrific panoramic viewpoint, with broad, interrupted views of the Lake District fells to one side and the open Irish Sea to the other. Try if you can to pick a clear day for the walk, when you should be able to see as far north as Scotland, as far south as Wales and as far west as the Isle of Man. The easy walking and fine views justify returning to Whicham by the same route as the climb up, but walkers who want more variety and distance can extend things via one of Wainwright's other suggested ascents, or add in one or both of his diversions, also noted in the directions.

Given its appeal, it is surprising to find that Black Combe is often deserted on days when much less satisfying fells in the central Lake District are packed. Its lonely location and relatively hard-to-reach starting point put many walkers off, but that just adds to the reasons to stride up. As Wainwright writes: 'Black Combe was made to be climbed, and climbed it should be.'

William Wordsworth was another fellwalker to be impressed. He wrote of it: 'This height a ministering angel might select/ For from the summit of Black Comb (dread name/ Derived from clouds and storms!) the amplest range/ Of unobstructed prospect may be seen/ That British ground commands. . . . In depth, in height, in circuit, how serene/ The spectacle, how pure! Of Nature's works/ In earth, and air, and earth-embracing sea/ A revelation infinite it seems/ Display august of man's inheritance/ Of Britain's calm felicity and power!'

From *The Outlying Fells of Lakeland*

Distance 5 miles (8km)

Ascent 1,850 feet (565m)

Start and finish point The lay-by with free parking for several cars near St Mary's church at Whicham on the A595 (SD 135 836)

Ordnance Survey maps Explorer OL6; Landranger 96

Getting there
The lay-by is directly off the A595, just before you reach its junction with the A5093 if driving from the east. Whicham is a small cluster of houses and can be easily missed, but look out for the parking spot as the church comes into view; if you reach the T-junction you have gone too far. The A595 connects major towns along the west coast of Cumbria, from Workington down to Barrow-in-Furness.

This is a good walk to start and finish by train. Silecroft is less than ½ mile (800m) from the starting point, and has a station on the scenic Cumbrian coast line, running from Carlisle down to Barrow-in-Furness. Trains run in either direction about once an hour from Monday to Saturday, but note that they do not run at all on Sundays. To get to the start of the walk from the tiny station at Silecroft, walk up to the A5093 and turn left along it, but very soon cross the road carefully and leave it to the right on a footpath signposted for Black Combe. It emerges on the A595; turn right along it for the lay-by, or cut out the stretch along the road by crossing it and taking the footpath on to the lane described in the directions.

Facilities, food and drink

The closest village with facilities to the start of the walk is Silecroft. The Miners Arms pub is right by the station; it serves decent food and is very family-friendly (01229 772325, www.minersarms-silecroft.co.uk). Other local pubs include the King William IV a mile to the south at Kirksanton (01229 772009). Millom, a couple of miles further on, has plenty more food and drink options, and things to see including the Millom Heritage Museum and Visitor Centre (01229 772555, www.millomfolkmuseum.co.uk).

The beaches at Silecroft and elsewhere along the coast are ideal for families, with wide expanses to play and picnic on, and there are rock pools after high tide. Other local attractions include Muncaster Castle, a 12-mile (19km) drive to the north, which has plenty of things for children to do (01229 717614, www.muncaster.co.uk). The well-kept St Mary's church right by the start of this walk is also worth a visit, especially for its modern stained glass windows.

Directions

1 Leave the lay-by on the public footpath, signposted for Whicham Church and Black Combe. The lane passes to the right of the church and then through a gap between the church and an old school building, now a home and craft shop, before dropping down some stone steps to another lane. Turn left along it and rise gently to a house, where you pick up a rougher track to curve behind the buildings.

2 Where the track runs out, leave it to the right on a footpath signposted for Black Coomb (one of several variations on the spelling of the fell). It soon passes through a wooden gate, and the path to the top of Black Combe is now clear, climbing steadily for most of the way. It first traverses a hill to the left, before pulling up to a flatter area (SD 131 838), from which Black Combe looms impressively into view ahead. After another pull up, the path traverses the heather-covered south-western flank of Black Combe, with views out to the open sea to your left. It then curves round to the north of the fell, regular cairns now accompanying the track. The summit itself is a little way off the main path, helpfully indicated by a large arrow made up of stones set into the grass. (There is an alternative way up to the top before the arrow, but avoid it as the short-cut erodes the fellside.) The summit is marked by an Ordnance Survey triangulation column (SD 135 855), surrounded by a stone shelter, which makes a welcome windbreak on the exposed and often chilly top. See Wainwright's notes on the fells you can see from here.

3 For a straightforward descent, retrace your steps back to Whicham. To extend the walk slightly, go east to Wainwright's suggested diversion to Blackcombe Screes – but keep a close eye on children near here. For the subsidiary top, walk for about 435 yards (400m) due south from the shelter, continuing over a depression with a small tarn to reach the cairns and more fine views. For a more substantial extension to the walk, you could continue on the main path over Black Combe, which descends to the north-west and then runs parallel with the A595 to Whitbeck. After a short stretch along the road you can pick up a footpath on the left back to Whicham.

Black Combe

We were brought up to believe that
the height of Black Combe was 1969'.
The Ordnance Survey have latterly
been suffering agonies of doubt and
now announce the altitude as

1970'

Well, let's have it right.

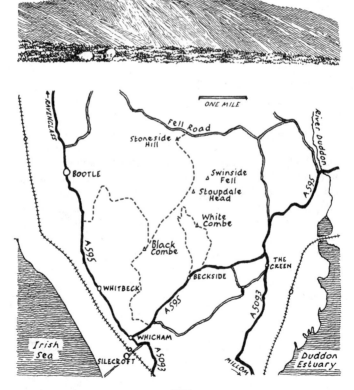

Visitors to Lakeland, especially if newly introduced to the district, often have difficulty in identifying many of the mountains by name, even distinctive ones such as Great Gable and Bowfell and Pillar assuming different shapes from unfamiliar angles.

But Black Combe is never confused with others. Although in fact linked with the main grouping of high fells by a continuous ridge it appears aloof, rising on the southern seaboard and overtopping all else like a huge whale stranded on a beach, a landmark visible over far distances and always unmistakeable. Because of its detachment Black Combe is rarely included by fellwalking visitors in their itineraries, yet is within the boundary of the National Park, which hereabouts coincides with the shoreline, and its ascent, in conditions of clear visibility, is one of the most rewarding. As a viewpoint it is unique. Half of the panorama is the glittering sea, with the Isle of Man seen in stark outline and the hills of Wales and Scotland as shadowy silhouettes on a high horizon of water. A fine array of mountains is the landward feature, the fells of southern Lakeland ranging across the scene and appearing, at this distance, in correct perspective, while round to the east the Pennines and the Bowland Fells form the background to a colourful landscape of undulating terrain pierced by long estuaries and dotted with scattered small towns and villages. The coast is seen, an unbroken line, from St. Bees Head to the Isle of Walney.

Black Combe and its satellites form a lofty mass between the valleys of the Duddon and the Esk. A single-track road and a few paths cross this wild upland. It is excellent territory for walking, with enough possible variations of routes to cater for a full week afoot.

Black Combe was made to be climbed, and climbed it should be. It is considerate to the old and infirm: the grass bridleway to its summit from Whicham is amongst the most delectable of Lakeland fell paths. Which other can be ascended in carpet slippers?

The start of the Whicham path
as seen from the church

Site of old copper mine,
Whitecombe Beck

The Whicham path at 1500'

right:
Whitecombe Screes

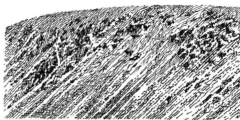

below:
Whicham Mill

Three routes of ascent are described, with maps, in the following pages: from south, west and north, the first two being on excellent continuous paths; and a fourth, from the east (via White Combe), is suggested. A defect of the first three is the lack of alternative routes of return to the startingpoint for walkers whose base is a parked car, but if use can be made of bus or train services or if a mutual arrangement can be made with another party of like ambition to exchange cars parked at different places, then a combination of routes is possible.

Allow four hours for any of the three direct routes (up and down) but more on days of clear visibility.

ASCENT FROM WHICHAM

5¼ miles
there and back

1900 feet of ascent including detours

The ascent of Black Combe from Whicham is the route most favoured, is without complications, and much the best: indeed the splendid path that directs the feet upwards to the very top, and the unparalleled views, make it a classic. The climb is unremitting, although easing midway, so that the amount of ascent between Whicham at 120 feet and the summit at 1970 is exactly 1850 feet, no more and no less; and the well-contrived cart-width path of dry turf makes every inch a delight. This path is not only the best way up but also the best way down and is recommended for use both ways with little detours on the summit. Walkers who object to treading the same ground twice can combine the route with one of the other three given, but in this case the Whicham path should be reserved for descent.

The start of this popular climb is marked by a layby and a signpost (to Whicham Church and Black Combe). From here the route follows a tarmac lane to the church and continues along a narrow passage between the churchyard and the former school, which is now a private house and craft shop. Then turn left along a tarmac lane to the house at its end, rounding the buildings by a walled track to the open fell. Cross the wire fence here (stile) and join and follow the grass path slanting up to the right. It would take a genius to go astray now. The path winds up unmistakeably, occasionally being bypassed where overgrown, and climbs to the top of the side-valley of Moorgill Beck, at 1000 feet, where the upper slopes of the fell come into view, with the path seen slanting left across the heathery dome. Extensive vistas east and west, ranging from the Pennines to the Isle of Man, also appear as the path continues, now less steeply. Higher, at 1850 feet, the path bends left and then right at a large arrow of stones laid out on the ground. At this point turn up right to the Ordnance column on the main top. A short detour eastwards to see Blackcombe Screes is recommended, followed by a visit to the lower south top for the prospect seawards. Return along the same path, again enjoying the fine views that endow Black Combe with a distinction not shared by other Lakeland fells.

Whicham Church
(St Mary's)

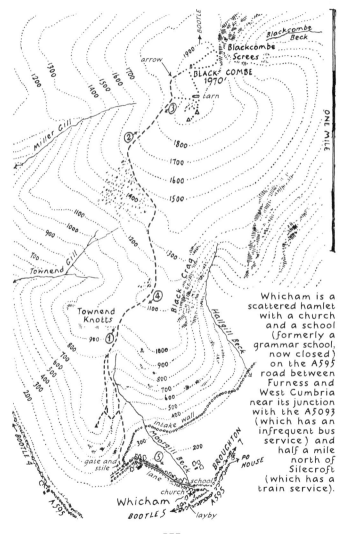

BOOTLE ↑

Blackcombe
Beck

arrow

Blackcombe
Screes

BLACK COMBE
1970'

ONE MILE

tarn

Miller Gill

②

1900

1800

1700

1600

1500

1400

1200
1300
1400
1500
1600
1700

1100
1000
900
700

Townend Gill

1200

1300

Black Crag

④

Hallgill Beck

Townend
Knotts

①

1100

1000

900

800

600
500
400
300

800
900
1000

700
600
500
400

Intake wall

Moorgill Beck

BROUGHTON

PO
HOUSE

200

300

200

⑤

gate and
stile

lane

school

church

Whicham

BOOTLE 4

A595

BOOTLE 5

A595

layby

Whicham is a
scattered hamlet
with a church
and a school
(formerly a
grammar school,
now closed)
on the A595
road between
Furness and
West Cumbria
near its junction
with the A5093
(which has an
infrequent bus
service) and
half a mile
north of
Silecroft
(which has a
train service).

177

ASCENT FROM HOLEGILL BRIDGE, BOOTLE
1950 feet of ascent   8 miles there and back

The bridleway up the western flank provides another well-graded and distinct route to the summit of Black Combe, easier even than the Whicham path but longer and more circuitous.

A bridleway runs along the western base of Black Combe by the intake wall and parallel to the main road. Reaching it from the road out of Bootle appears to be legitimate only at one point: by public footpath 300 yards south of Holegill Bridge at a gate directly opposite a lane to Barfield and adjacent to a tree-shadowed ruin where there is parking space for one car (there is better parking north of the bridge). The walk is deemed to start here and miles are measured on the map from this point. From the gate a track goes alongside a wall and emerges, after two more gates, onto the bridleway. Turn left, crossing over Holegill Beck (which is difficult, but not impossible). Now all is plain sailing. Follow the intake wall to the ruins of Hall Foss, where the bridleway turns uphill by a wall succeeded by a fence. (The short cut to the right is only useful in descent.) The path swings right on the brow of the hill (view forward here to the Pillar range). The only further direction necessary is to keep the bridleway underfoot:

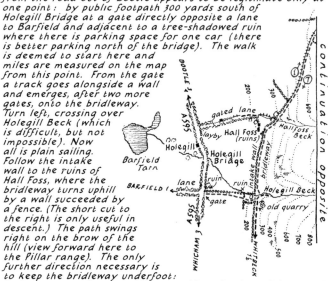

it is grassy, of cart width, provides simple walking, and, although circuitous, cleverly avoiding all depressions, leads unerringly to the top of Black Combe (and continues, with a break, down to Whicham). The surroundings on this ascent are tedious but relieved by the distant views. On the summit, where there is an Ordnance Survey column, visit the rim of the Screes, and, if visibility is good, the lower south top.

The finest descent, unquestionably, is down the bridleway to Whicham, and this is where the non-car-owner scores if he can arrange his times to catch a bus back to Bootle. Otherwise return by the route of ascent. A short cut by William Gill and Holegill Beck, saving a mile, is obvious, but the walking, through lush pastures of bilberry, and lower down steep bracken, is slow compared with the bridleway, along which a spanking pace can be worked up and the car reached in an hour, although a leisurely saunter is preferable.

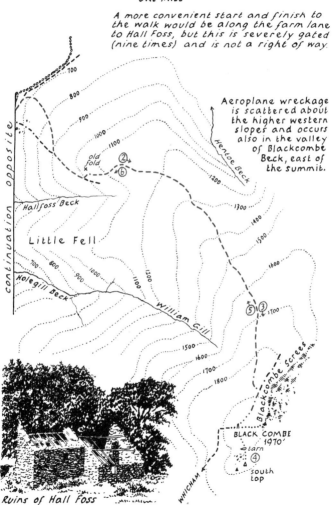

ONE MILE

A more convenient start and finish to
the walk would be along the farm lane
to Hall Foss, but this is severely gated
(nine times) and is not a right of way.

Aeroplane wreckage
is scattered about
the higher western
slopes and occurs
also in the valley
of Blackcombe
Beck, east of
the summit.

continuation opposite

Hentoe Beck

old
fold
×

②→
←⑥

Hallfoss Beck

Little Fell

Holegill Beck

William Gill

700 800 900 1000 1100 1200

1300

1400

1500

1600

⑤ ③
←⑦ 1700

1500

1600

1700

1800

Blackcombe Screes

WHICHAM

BLACK COMBE
1970'

tarn

④

south
top

Ruins of Hall Foss

ASCENT FROM THE FELL ROAD
1350 feet of ascent

7 miles
there and back

Ancient limbs will respond more readily to the route to Black Combe from the top of the fell road, this, at 1300 feet, giving a good 'leg up' for walkers with cars, and the climbing, furthermore, being of easy gradient. It is, however, a tedious approach and rather marred by a bad swamp that must be faced twice, there being no alternative way back to the car. But if a plan can be devised for sending the car round to await you at Whicham Church or arrangements made for a mutual exchange of cars with someone of like ambition, this line of ascent combined with a descent to Whicham makes a splendid traverse of Black Combe from end to end.

There is car-parking space at the summit of the fell road on the south side. Black Combe is in view here, to the left of the prominent Stoneside Hill, a rough little eminence crossed by an old wall. This is the first objective. On the far side there is an unfortunate loss of height to a swamp in a depression. Cross it gingerly; wet feet are inevitable. Then climb the easy slope beyond, crossing the fence by a stile, and so arrive on the indefinite top of Stoupdale Head. (A short detour left here brings the valley of Stoupdale into view directly below, and away to the left in the next valley, the stone circle at Swinside can be discerned).

Black Combe looms ahead. Aim for it across a depression and follow the edge of Whitecombe Screes and Blackcombe Screes, above a deep valley on the left, to the summit. If time and energy permit, visit the south top also. Failing a car-swap with a friend coming up from Whicham (whose arrival on the summit should coincide with yours), return to the fell road by the same route, deviating only to skirt round the top of Stoneside Hill.

Stoupdale Head and Black Combe, from Stoneside Hill

MAP

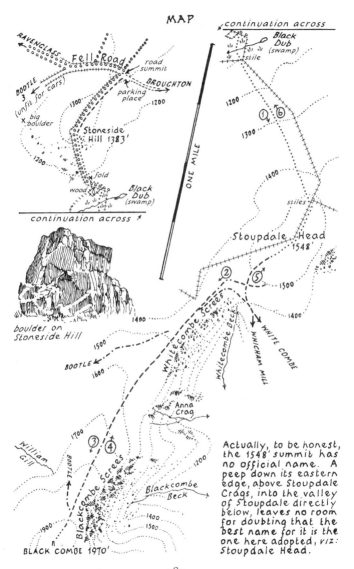

Actually, to be honest, the 1548' summit has no official name. A peep down its eastern edge, above Stoupdale Crags, into the valley of Stoupdale directly below, leaves no room for doubting that the best name for it is the one here adopted, viz: Stoupdale Head.

ASCENT OF WHITE COMBE FROM BECKSIDE

1250 feet of ascent

4½ miles

3 hours

White Combe is a buttress of Black Combe on the east side, separated by a valley but with a high-level link. It makes a fine walk, returning down the valley, and can conveniently be used as a stepping-stone to its bigger neighbour.

From its junction with the side-road to Ralliss go along the A595 east for a third of a mile until, on a bend, a gated lane between hedges branches off on the left: it is a public footpath but has the appearance of a virgin jungle. A safari along it leads to a gate giving access to the open fell, a sea of bracken, which is bisected by a deep groove (a drove road) slanting up to the right: a track runs alongside. Follow this. Beyond a left-hand bend it becomes indistinct on easier ground, then re-appears to skirt the slopes of White Combe, the summit of which is reached by a simple climb up to the left and found to be crowned with a great heap of stones like a tumulus and fashioned into a wind-shelter. Then, for an alternative route of return, aim northwest along the level ridge to meet another drove road descending into the deep valley on the left. Follow this down, enjoying intimate views of the rough recesses of Black Combe and passing two heaps of spoil remaining from copper-mine operations, to the intake wall at the foot of the valley, where a track in pleasant wooded surroundings leads down to Whicham Mill (now an attractive cottage) and, becoming a tarmac road, continues past Ralliss to the A595.

The summit of White Combe
looking to Stoupdale Head

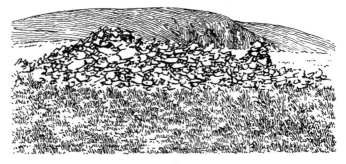

MAP

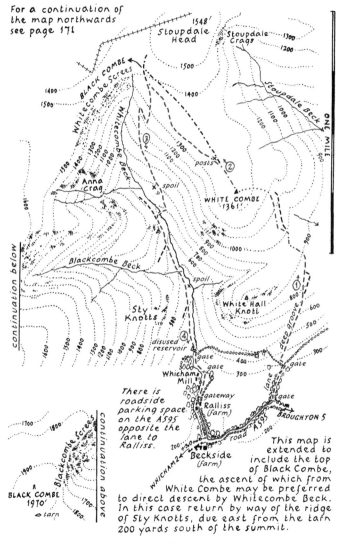

For a continuation of the map northwards see page 171

1548'
Stoupdale Head

Stoupdale Crags

BLACK COMBE Screes

Whitecombe Screes

Whitecombe Beck

Stoupdale Beck

ONE MILE

③

posts

②

Anna Crag

WHITE COMBE
1361'

continuation below

Blackcombe Beck

Sty Knotts

spoil

spoil

White Hall Knott

①

disused reservoir

④

lane deep groove

gate

gate

gate

gate

Whicham Mill

gateway

Ralliss (farm)

gate

BROUGHTON 5

There is roadside parking space on the A595 opposite the lane to Ralliss.

road

A595

continuation above

Black combe Screes

BLACK COMBE 1970'

tarn

WHICHAM

Beckside (farm)

This map is extended to include the top of Black Combe, the ascent of which from White Combe may be preferred to direct descent by Whitecombe Beck. In this case return by way of the ridge of Sly Knotts, due east from the tarn 200 yards south of the summit.

183

The summit, a beacon site, is a smooth grassy plateau, so flat that the Ordnance column and its walled surround cannot be seen until the last few moments of ascent; in fact there are football grounds with playing surfaces a lot worse than the top of Black Combe. A short stroll eastwards leads to the striking downfall of Blackcombe Screes, a steep craggy declivity forming the mountain's best feature. South of the main summit and beyond a depression containing a tarn is a subsidiary top with a well-built cairn and a pile of stones indicating better viewpoints for the extensive seascape and coastline.

Just to make sure you have climbed the right fell check the number of the Ordnance column. If it is 11602 your orienteering has been impeccable.

Cairns on the south top

Furness Peninsula   Barrow   Isle of Walney

Duddon Estuary

184

Blackcombe Screes

above: *looking north to Buck Barrow*
            and Whitfell
below: *looking south*

The Lakeland Skyline

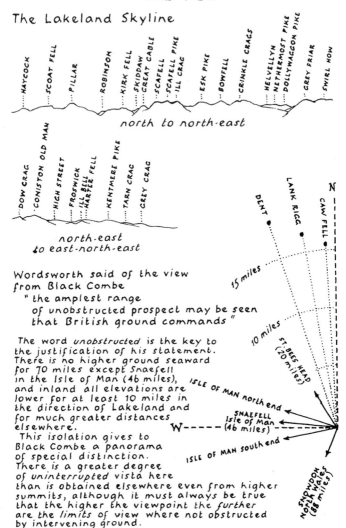

HAYCOCK · SCOAT FELL · PILLAR · ROBINSON · KIRK FELL · SKIDDAW · GREAT GABLE · SCAFELL · SCAFELL PIKE · ILL CRAG · ESK PIKE · BOWFELL · CRINKLE CRAGS · HELVELLYN · NETHERMOST PIKE · DOLLYWAGGON PIKE · GREY FRIAR · SWIRL HOW

north to north-east

DOW CRAG · CONISTON OLD MAN · HIGH STREET · FROSWICK · ILL BELL · HARTER FELL · KENTMERE PIKE · TARN CRAG · GREY CRAG

north-east to east-north-east

Wordsworth said of the view from Black Combe

" the amplest range of unobstructed prospect may be seen that British ground commands "

The word *unobstructed* is the key to the justification of his statement. There is no higher ground seaward for 70 miles except Snaefell in the Isle of Man (46 miles), and inland all elevations are lower for at least 10 miles in the direction of Lakeland and for much greater distances elsewhere.

This isolation gives to Black Combe a panorama of special distinction. There is a greater degree of uninterrupted vista here than is obtained elsewhere even from higher summits, although it must always be true that the higher the viewpoint the further are the *limits* of view where not obstructed by intervening ground.

DENT · LANK RIGG · CAW FELL · N

15 miles

10 miles

ST. BEES HEAD (20 miles)

ISLE OF MAN north end

SNAEFELL Isle of Man (46 miles)

W

ISLE OF MAN south end

SNOWDON NORTH WALES (88 miles)

The high ground of Lakeland fits neatly into the sector between north (map north not magnetic north) and east-north-east. The array of mountains is splendid but is confined almost entirely to those in the southern part of the district. As a viewpoint of Lakeland Black Combe is much inferior to many other elevations, Skiddaw Little Man (the best of all) for instance. Nevertheless the prospect is one of great charm, the Esk and Duddon valleys leading the eye to a concentration of noble peaks.

Principal Fells

N

SKIDDAW

HAYCOCK
SCOAT FELL
PILLAR
ROBINSON
KIRK FELL
GREAT GABLE
SCAFELL PIKE
ILL CRAG
ESK PIKE
BOWFELL
CRINKLE CRAGS

HELVELLYN PIKE
DOLLYWAGGON PIKE
DOLLERMOST PIKE

25 miles

20 miles

HIGH STREET
ILL BELL
HARTER FELL
KENTMERE PIKE
TARN CRAG
GREY CRAG

GREY FRIAR
SWIRL HOW
DOW CRAG
CONISTON OLD MAN

BUCK BARROW
WHITFELL
HESK FELL
GREEN CRAG
HARTER
FELLS
STICKLE
CAW

WOODLAND FELL
TOP O' SELSIDE

BLAWITH KNOTT

GUMMERS HOW

BURNEY

E

INGLEBOROUGH (38 miles)

BARROW IN FURNESS
ISLE OF WALNEY

As a place for appraising the coastal plain and estuaries, however, Black Combe is quite supreme. Thirty continuous miles of shoreline and its pleasant hinterland are seen as on a map. The towns and villages fit unobtrusively into a tranquil scene. The one jarring feature is the atomic power station, spoiling the prospect of the Esk estuary and the sands of Ravenglass.

16 Whitbarrow
from Mill Side

Wainwright liked Whitbarrow so much that he singled it out as 'the most beautiful in this book [*The Outlying Fells of Lakeland*]; beautiful it is every step of the way.' Given that the book has fifty-six walks, and that Wainwright never dished out these sort of accolades lightly, this is high praise indeed.

Whitbarrow is a delightful walk and very suitable for families, with the walking underfoot easy and all the climbing got out of the way over the first few miles. The traverse of Whitbarrow Scar is exhilarating, with great views on all sides and much of its length dramatically wild and exposed, though heather, bracken and windblown saplings interrupt the jagged outcrops to make a real patchwork of a top.

The distinctive scar, which is visible for miles around, is made up of carboniferous limestone, which used to be mined for use in building and agriculture but is now protected by its designated status as both a national nature reserve and site of special scientific interest. The limestone fosters some unusual plant and grass species as well as rare butterflies, birds and sometimes deer, and there is something special to see for most of the year, though it is at its best in high summer. The Cumbria Wildlife Trust helps to look after the area, and has more information about what to look out for on the way over the Scar (015398 16300, www.cumbriawildlifetrust.org.uk).

This walk can be shortened by following one of Wainwright's two suggested alternatives, or by arranging to be picked up from the road at North Lodge, as indicated in the directions – though this last option misses out on much of the fine return to Witherslack, with the cover of trees making for a nice contrast to the exposed expanse of the summit ridge.

From *The Outlying Fells of Lakeland*

Distance 6½ miles (10.5km)

Ascent 800 feet (245m)

Start and finish point The mill pond at Mill Side near Witherslack (SD 448 842)

Ordnance Survey maps Explorer OL7; Landranger 96

Getting there

Mill Side is just off the A590, the mostly dual carriageway linking the M6 and Barrow-in-Furness. Take the first Witherslack turn-off if you are driving from the Kendal side, and look for parking spaces on the short drive up to Mill Side; there are lay-bys both close to the A590 and further up towards the hamlet.

The X35 bus stops close to the start of the walk, and runs every hour between Kendal and Barrow-in-Furness. If you are getting off the bus from the Kendal direction, take great care crossing the A590 and walk up the much quieter road to the starting point in Mill Side; it is about ¼ mile (400m). The nearest train stations are in Kendal and Grange-over-Sands, both of which connect to the turn-off via the X35 bus.

Facilities, food and drink

The nearest facilities are in Witherslack, about a mile (1.6km) south-west of Mill Side. You can walk or drive to the village along a quiet road that runs parallel to the A590. It has a very good community-run shop that sells excellent local produce and is well worth supporting (015395 52188; closed on Sundays). Very close by is the excellent Derby Arms pub, which serves good food at lunchtimes and evenings and all day on Sunday, and is family-friendly (015395 52207, www.thederbyarms.co.uk). There are more good pubs further east along the A590 at the turn-off for the A5074 (The Gilpin Bridge Inn; 015395 52206, www.gilpinbridgeinn.co.uk) and at Levens (The Hare and Hounds; 015395 60408, www.hareandhoundslevens.co.uk).

A unique feature of this walk is the Hikers' Rest (www.hikersrest.blogspot.com) – a delightful tiny café in a converted barn at Beck Head near the start and finish point that provides tea and cakes to walkers coming down off Whitbarrow. It is open round the clock and works on an honesty basis, with walkers invited to make their own drinks and leave their money in the envelopes provided in return. There are tables and chairs and a toilet inside, and word of mouth about the lovely idea has helped interest in the café to spread among Lake District walkers. It makes an ideal conclusion to the walk; see the notes in the directions to find it.

Directions

1 From the mill pond, take the narrow road signposted for Beck Head, immediately passing phone and post boxes and bearing right at the fork a few paces beyond. As the road climbs steeply, Whitbarrow Scar looms in front of you. The road dwindles into a track and levels out. 220 yards (200m) after it does so, leave it to the left on a path up through the trees, marked by a permissive footpath sign. It climbs sharply at first but soon levels out, the direction marked by white arrows.

2 At a bench (with nice views over Morecambe Bay and, unfortunately, the A590 too), a white arrow points left; follow it to climb again. The path passes through a gap in a wall and a small wooden gate in quick succession – as Wainwright notes, you could divert from the gate to see the Foulshaw Moss nature reserve – and then emerges from the trees on to the exposed top of Whitbarrow Scar. It goes on to reach a cairn (SD 449 853).

3 More large cairns are visible ahead of you from here. Follow the clear path towards them, passing over a wall stile a few hundred metres after the first. In all, it is nearly 1½ miles (2.4km) of wonderful ridge walking to the second, column cairn which marks Lord's Seat, the summit of Whitbarrow

(SD 442 871). There is no seat but great views all around; see Wainwright's notes for details of what you can see and the story behind the column's plaque.

4 Continue on from Lord's Seat, but after 75 yards (70m) leave the main path on a fainter one to the left, making for the right-hand edge of the trees in the distance, and ignoring a side path on the right a little further on. The path approaches then skirts the edge of the trees before approaching a wall. Just before it, at a junction of paths, bend left. This path drops steeply down the edge of a small scree gully – take care here, especially in the wet – and passes through a small wooden gate at the bottom of it. Continue down through the trees to reach a path crossroads and signpost (SD 435 877).

5 Turn right here, following the sign for North Lodge. The path drops down to a wall and bends left through the woods for about ½ mile (800m) to a road. (There is parking here, so anyone who wants to end the walk and can arrange a lift can do so here.) Turn left down the quiet, narrow road for about 1 mile (1.6km), passing, on your left, a tarn with Witherslack Hall (now a boarding and day school for boys) beyond it, and then an equestrian centre. After the centre, where the road bends right, leave it to the left on a lane downhill, signposted for Whitbarrow (SD 437 859).

6 Drop down to a wooden gate and cross the open field beyond, bearing half left in the direction of the footpath sign, with the spectacular sheer cliffs of Chapel Head Scar ahead. Cross a gate and stile at the edge of the wood, and bear half right on the path ahead, which winds pleasantly through the wood for 1 mile (1.6km). At a junction of paths at the end of the wood, turn left. You soon reach the pretty hamlet of Beck Head and, in the farm buildings on your right, the Hikers' Rest honesty café (SD 445 847). Follow the road down for nearly ½ mile (800m) back to the mill pond at Mill Side.

Whitbarrow

visiting
Lord's Seat 706'

800 feet of ascent

Pool Bank
Lord's Seat
Whitbarrow
Hall
Church
Witherslack
Mill Side
Town End
LEVENS BRIDGE
GRANGE A590
ONE MILE

Mill Side

192

Whitbarrow is an abrupt ridge of limestone on a north-south axis soaring boldly above the flat marshes and mosses of the Kent Estuary and is a parallel counterpart to the long cliff of Scout Scar across the alluvial valley of Lyth. Rich woodlands clothe the lower slopes and in the east pine plantations climb almost to the summit. To the west a four-mile escarpment extends along the crest like a castle wall and is repeated on a smaller scale at the highest limits of the eastern forests. But the spine of the ridge is bare, although 'bare' is an inapt word for the wealth of heather and bracken, juniper and saplings that form so colourful a carpet. In places this carpet has worn thin, revealing a naked surface of patchy scree and outcrops of dazzling whiteness.

Whitbarrow's delights of plant and wild life have been recognised by the adoption in 1969 of its summit plateau as a nature reserve, and there is nowhere a more attractive landscape in which to enjoy the manifold pleasures of a natural environment allied to a far-reaching and very lovely panorama.

The walk described is the most beautiful in this book; beautiful it is every step of the way. It includes a traverse of the finest part of the scar top and returns through delightful woods along the base of the cliffs. After initial steepness the walking is exceedingly pleasant, in surroundings high above encircling valleys and amidst scenery that has no blemish. All is fair to the eye on Whitbarrow.

looking north
to Lord's Seat

The Nature Reserve

The Lake District Naturalists' Trust was formed in 1962 largely as a result of the efforts of Canon G.A.K. Hervey, and after his death in 1967 an inspired proposal to acquire Flodder Allotment (the walled enclosure including Lord's Seat on the highest part of Whitbarrow) as a memorial to him was happily brought to fruition. The area was declared a nature reserve in 1969, a visible recognition of the Canon's services to the Trust being accorded by a tablet built into a fine cairn on Lord's Seat and inscribed as follows:

This Reserve
Commemorates
CANON G.A.K. HERVEY
1893 - 1967
Founder of the
Lake District Naturalists' Trust

The emblem of the Trust

Lonely Whitbarrow, remote from urban influences, is the last place one would associate with industrial exploitation, and it is strange to find in a corner of Flodder Allotment the scanty but obvious remains of a drift mine, with an open level still penetrating deep into the fellside — the sort of place readers of this book would have enjoyed exploring in their heyday, but not now.

The nature of the spoil suggests that iron was extracted.

Chapel Head
Scar

Beck Head

Mill Side is an outpost of Witherslack a third of a mile off the Grange–Levens Bridge road (A590), and is a pleasant hamlet with a mill-pond, now attractively incorporated into a number of private gardens. From the pond take the road signposted to Beck Head and bear right at the fork, past a farmyard, heading for the vertical end of Whitbarrow Scar, which dominates this rural scene. At the top of the hill the road bends right at a signpost and levels out. In 200 yards ascend a thin path branching left into the woodland until an old seat is reached at the foot of a pine tree. At this point exactly, turn sharp left on a higher path above the line of approach to a gap in a wall on the top of the Scar. The gap is immediately succeeded by a small gate on the right, giving access to an indistinct path through woodland. (A diversion here is worth while: instead of turning right through the gate continue along the wall to a viewpoint where the raised bog of Foulshaw Moss is seen as from an aeroplane. The bog was acquired in 1998 by the Cumbria Wildlife Trust, who felled all the conifers and made it into a nature reserve.) Soon the path becomes clearer and the trees become more scattered. The path climbs gradually to a cairned summit, from which point the full length of the traverse of the scar top to the furthest cairn in sight, on Lord's Seat, can be surveyed. Go forward over an intermediate summit (large cairn), and continue to a stile in a cross-wall ahead, where a path will be found leading onwards along the base of a continuous escarpment on the right, the delightful surroundings being akin to a natural rock garden. Soon the path leaves the escarpment and heads unerringly for the well-made cairn on Lord's Seat, which is centred in an interesting limestone landscape and has good distant views. Rest awhile here, keeping your chest well covered up if there is a breeze, and then proceed north. Don't take the obvious path, but a fainter one farther left, and bear left in a hundred yards onto a path that is easily missed and leads to an old mine level. Turn left here, descending sharply on the fringe of a scree slope to a gate in a wall, where a sign of the Cumbria Wildlife Trust is affixed. The path goes roughly into the wood, becoming easier at the foot of the slope. Ignore paths branching left and right and go on ahead through the wood, the path becoming a cart-track before emerging on a tarmac road. Turn left along this quiet road, a lovely avenue of trees, getting a splendid glimpse of the stately pile of Witherslack Hall. An equestrian centre is passed, and at the bottom of the short hill beyond (adjoining the main entrance-drive to the Hall), turn left along a lane, passing farm buildings, into an open field with the very impressive cliffs of Chapel Head Scar ahead. Cross the field, bearing slightly left, to a gate on the edge of the wood below the cliffs. Through it, turn right on a wide path amidst trees for a full mile to emerge on a lane near Beck Head, which, followed to the left, returns you to Mill Side. The final delight of the route is the remarkable resurgence at the base of a low cliff by the roadside that gives the lovely hamlet of Beck Head its name.

MAP

The full route as described opposite may be overlong for octogenarians and upwards, who, instead, may make two shorter walks out of it:

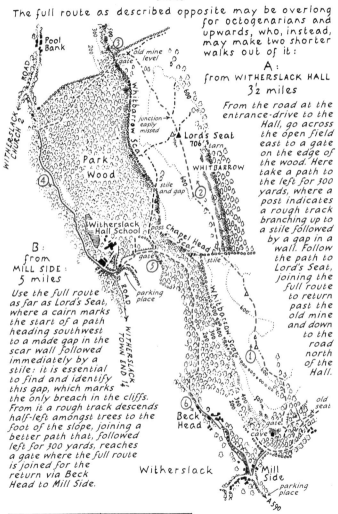

A:
from WITHERSLACK HALL
3½ miles

From the road at the entrance-drive to the Hall, go across the open field east to a gate on the edge of the wood. Here take a path to the left for 300 yards, where a post indicates a rough track branching up to a stile followed by a gap in a wall. Follow the path to Lord's Seat, joining the full route to return past the old mine and down to the road north of the Hall.

B:
from MILL SIDE:
5 miles

Use the full route as far as Lord's Seat, where a cairn marks the start of a path heading southwest to a made gap in the scar wall followed immediately by a stile: it is essential to find and identify this gap, which marks the only breach in the cliffs. From it a rough track descends half-left amongst trees to the foot of the slope, joining a better path that, followed left for 300 yards, reaches a gate where the full route is joined for the return via Beck Head to Mill Side.

Pool Bank

WITHERSLACK CHURCH 2

ROAD

Whitbarrow Scar

old mine level

gate

junction easily missed

Lord's Seat 706' cairn

WHITBARROW

Park Wood

stile and gap

Witherslack Hall School

post Chapel Head Scar

gate

parking place

ROAD

WITHERSLACK TOWN END 1½

Whitbarrow Scars

stile

old seat

Beck Head

cave

gate

Witherslack

Mill Side

parking place

A590

ONE MILE

197

17 Muncaster Fell
from Muncaster Castle

Like many of the summits in this book, Muncaster Fell delivers views that far outweigh the effort required to reach them. The highest point is barely 750 feet, yet its raised, isolated position between Miterdale and Eskdale makes for outstanding panoramic views, both out across the coast and inland to the fells. It is also a very good introduction to the far western fringes of the Lake District, an area that feels wilder and more desolate than the central region. As a result, it is also much less trodden than many fells, and on days out of high season you may well have it to yourself – though the Sellafield nuclear power station, visible from points along the walk, is a rather stark reminder that you are not quite alone.

Apart from a few boggy stretches, the going underfoot along this walk is easy, and the climbing is steady rather than steep. It starts by rising up a lane – following the course of an old Roman road that once connected Ravenglass to the fort on Hardknott Pass – and then pulling up to Hooker Crag, the highest point on the fell. It then traverses the length of the ridge, which makes for a wonderful couple of miles walking that children will enjoy leading, before descending to return through woodland back to the lane and Muncaster Castle. If you can, combine the walk with a visit to the Castle and a ride on the Ravenglass and Eskdale railway, both very popular attractions for families and described in more detail below.

It is hard to believe Muncaster Fell is not more popular among walkers – but take advantage of the fact and enjoy its splendid isolation. As Wainwright puts it: 'Here is enchantment.'

From *The Outlying Fells of Lakeland*

Distance 7 miles (11.3km)

Ascent 750 feet (230m)

Start and finish point The large free car park opposite the main entrance to Muncaster Castle (SD 098 967). It is intended for visitors to the castle or its grounds, so buy a ticket and enjoy it before or after the walk. There is a lay-by with free parking for several cars about 65 yards (60m) eastwards from the car park on the A595

Ordnance Survey maps Explorer OL6; Landranger 96

Getting there
Muncaster Castle is on the A595, the long road that links together towns along the west coast of Cumbria, from Workington in the north to near Barrow-in-Furness. Muncaster Castle is signposted from both directions.

The number 6 bus terminates at the Muncaster Castle car park, stopping at towns including Whitehaven, Egremont, Gosforth and Seascale on the way, though there are only a few services a day so check times carefully in advance. On Sundays it is replaced by the X6 service, which also connects to Barrow-in-Furness to the south, as well as other towns in between.

Ravenglass, less than a mile away to the west, is on the wonderful Cumbrian coast line, linking Carlisle and Barrow-in-Furness. Walk east towards and then along the A595 to reach the starting point, or follow Wainwright's footpath diversion in his notes. The train station is also one terminus of the scenic Ravenglass and Eskdale railway, which runs parallel with the Muncaster Fell ridge on your left-hand side as you traverse it. You can halve the length of this walk by using the railway to return to Ravenglass from Irton Road station at the point indicated in the directions. It is a request stop, so make sure the driver can spot you (01229 717171, www.ravenglass-railway.co.uk).

Facilities, food and drink

Muncaster Castle is well worth a visit either side of the walk, and is particularly good for children (01229 717614, www.muncaster.co.uk). As well as the historic and allegedly haunted house, lived in by the same family since the thirteenth century, it has splendid 70-acre grounds with family attractions including two playgrounds, a maze and picnic area. It is also home to the World Owl Centre, with 200 birds of prey on show, and has a nice café named after a resident ghost, Creeping Kate's Kitchen, plus various forms of accommodation. Everything is open every day from April to October, though the castle is often closed on Saturdays for weddings, and hours are more restricted in the winter, though the grounds are usually open.

Beyond the castle, food and drink can be had in the village of Ravenglass. As well as rides on the railway, the station has a good café and play area and its own pub, the Ratty Arms.

Directions

1 Turn left out of the car park and walk eastwards along the A595. The road soon rises and bends sharply right; leave it to the left here, on the right bridleway of two, signposted for Muncaster Fell via Fell Lane. The clear track, Fell Lane, rises gently and, after about ¾ mile (1.2km), descends slightly to an open area with signs of tree felling. At the fork of paths here, take the right-hand one. This rises again, soon passing a tarn on your left (Muncaster Tarn) and arriving at a wooden gate (SD 108 978).

2 Continue ahead, and look on the horizon for the Ordnance Survey cairn on the top of Hooker Crag; your next target. See Wainwright's notes for the other fells in view from here. There are alternative paths at first, but they soon join up, and the grassy path to Hooker Crag is then clear. Leave it to climb a few steps up to the cairn for great views (SD 112 983).

3 Continue on and descend to rejoin the main path, which continues along the length of Muncaster Fell. It can get boggy in places after rain, but you should be able to pick your way around the wetter patches. After about ½ mile (800m) it reaches a large boulder with more fine views. (As Wainwright notes, a short detour from here leads you to Ross's Camp, probably used by Victorian visitors as a picnic spot.) It then descends to a gate at the corner of a dry stone wall (SD 122 989). Take care over the marshy area before the gate, and skirt it to the left if you prefer.

4 The path beyond the gate stays close to the wall on your left at first, then bends away from it, passing a craggy hill, Silver Knott, to your left. About 1 mile (1.6km) on from the gate, it reaches another one, also at the corner of a dry stone wall. Go through and cross the enclosed area ahead to another gate in a wall. Ahead of this, the path becomes a track down to Muncaster Head Farm. (To divert to Irton Road station on the Ravenglass and Eskdale railway, follow the signpost from here.) Pass the farm buildings on your right, and reach a more defined lane by the farmhouse (SD 140 989).

5 Turn right along the lane, soon passing through a metal gate. The clear lane continues for 1½ miles (2.4km), with trees to either side for much of the distance, to reach a road at High Eskholme (SD 118 979). Continue along the road for about 220 yards (200m), then leave it on a gravel track to the right, indicated by public bridleway arrows. The path rises steadily, soon picking up a wall on your left. After ½ mile (800m), look out beyond the wall for houses and the monument described and sketched by Wainwright in his notes.

6 After another rise beyond that, pass through a wooden gate and continue on the path ahead. It soon returns you to the path followed earlier, just in front of Muncaster Tarn (SD 106 976). Turn left and soon reach the junction of paths at the open area. Take the left-hand path back down Fell Lane to the road, and turn left for the car park.

Muncaster Fell

Hooker Crag 757'

750 feet of ascent

Not named on some editions
of the 1" Ordnance map.

from
MUNCASTER CASTLE
CAR PARK

7¼ miles

5 hours

Hooker Crag

Muncaster Fell is a lowly height that yet contrives to
give an impression of much greater stature, especially
when viewed from the miniature railway along its base
where the rough craggy flank seems unassailable. Its
situation, isolated between
the flats of Miterdale
and Eskdale, is
magnificent,
commanding
a panorama
of great charm
both seawards and
inland to the mountains
of Lakeland. Heather
and bilberry, gorse and
bracken, woodland and
forest, lay a rich carpet of
colour over its slopes. But
the supreme joy of Muncaster
Fell is the delectable traverse of
its ridge, as described in the pages
following. Here is enchantment.

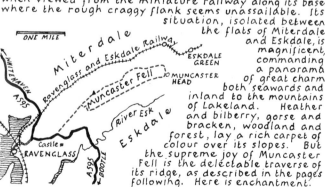

Muncaster Castle

Muncaster Castle, situated on a wooded hill enjoying a lovely view of Eskdale that inspired Ruskin to describe it as "the gateway to Paradise", occupies the location of a Roman tower. and dates from the 13th. century although extensively enlarged in more recent times. Its gardens are renowned for their exotic rhododendrons, camellias and azaleas. It is the seat of the Pennington family.

The summit of Muncaster Fell

Ross's Camp

Despite its name and its neolithic appearance
this miniature man-made Stonehenge has no
military or archaeological significance. It
is a monument only to the physical strength
of members of a Victorian shooting party who
raised the massive flat slab onto other stones
to serve as a luncheon table. The top of the
slab is neatly inscribed ROSS'S CAMP 1883.

Miterdale and Scafell from Muncaster Fell

There is a large car-park opposite the main entrance to Muncaster Castle (provided free for the use of visitors to the castle), and just east of it, by a telephone box, is a layby available to all. From here walk Bootlewards along the A595 and up a gentle rise to a sharp angle in the road, where two bridleways leave in the corner. Take the one signposted to Muncaster Fell via Fell Lane: this starts as a good straight cart-track up a leafy avenue between walls and rampant vegetation. Ignore a woodland path branching off to the right, and when the track divides in a depression bear right. A half-hidden tarn amid trees is glimpsed as the track resumes its uphill journey to a gate in a fence, and before long a fine view unfolds. Directly ahead is seen the Ordnance column on Hooker Crag, with the Pillar group to its left and Scafell, Bowfell and Co. to its right. The atomic power station is also unfortunately in sight northwest. The track goes forward under a line of pylons with a fence (enclosing a former plantation) alongside on the left: when this turns away a thin trod branches off the bridleway (now actually a public footpath) and leads pleasantly to the Ordnance column (No. S.5763) in a sea of bracken. The view is now extensive and uninterrupted by higher ground: it ranges from the Isle of Man to Black Combe, the skyline including the Pillar, Scafell, Bowfell and Coniston groups. The path descends beyond the column to cross a flat depression and leads eventually to a large rounded boulder, another fine viewpoint with a charming prospect of Miterdale and Eskdale. Looking back to the right from here (in the direction of Black Combe) you can see Ross's Camp, which may be visited by a short detour. Beyond the boulder the path descends steeply and the gateway that is your next objective can be seen ahead beyond a marshy area that is best skirted to the left. From the gateway the path continues downhill (rather wet), inclining across a depression on the right. A slight rise is followed by a long descent, the path here being retained by a granite wall. A gate in a crosswall ahead is used to continue forward in a surround of rich vegetation to another wall and a gate. A cart-track here goes down to the farm of Muncaster Head: pass through three gates to the right of the buildings to reach the farm access lane. Turn right along this for 1½ pleasantly wooded miles to High Eskholme, where tarmac appears, and, a furlong beyond, leave it at a gap on the right, which admits to a bridleway rising distinctly through a mature plantation with a wall on the left. In about half a mile a house comes into view over the wall, followed by the monument illustrated overleaf. There are still plants growing out of its roof. The bridleway eventually rejoins the outward route at the tarn. If use has been made of the car park one should perhaps purchase a ticket to enter the castle grounds, which are well worth a visit. Among the features are a world owl centre, a meadow vole maze, Himalayan gardens, a wildlife pond, a dragonfly pool and a plant centre.

A map of the route is given overleaf →

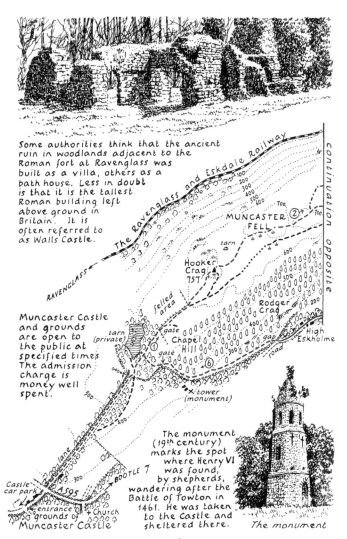

Some authorities think that the ancient ruin in woodlands adjacent to the Roman fort at Ravenglass was built as a villa, others as a bath house. Less in doubt is that it is the tallest Roman building left above ground in Britain. It is often referred to as Walls Castle.

The Ravenglass and Eskdale Railway

RAVENGLASS

continuation opposite

MUNCASTER FELL ②

tarn

Hooker Crag 757

300
400
500
700
600

felled area

Rodger Crag

High Eskholme

gate
tarn (private) ①

gate ①

Chapel Hill

gap

road

⑥

Muncaster Castle and grounds are open to the public at specified times. The admission charge is money well spent.

500

x tower (monument)

400

lane

300

Castle car park

A595

BOOTLE 7

entrance to grounds of Muncaster Castle

+ Church

The monument (19th century) marks the spot where Henry VI was found, by shepherds, wandering after the Battle of Towton in 1461. He was taken to the Castle and sheltered there.

The monument

206

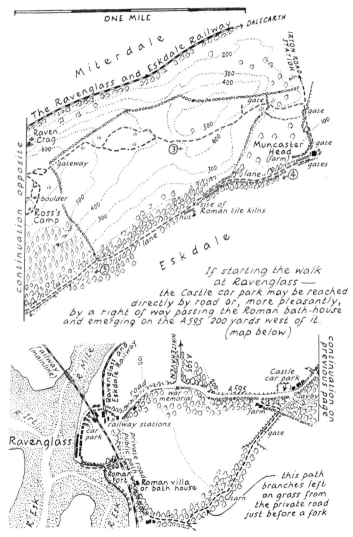

MAP

ONE MILE

Miterdale

The Ravenglass and Eskdale Railway → DALECARTH

IRTON ROAD STATION

200

300

400

Raven Crag

600

gateway

500

400

③

500

400

300

gate

gate

Muncaster Head (farm)

100

gate

gates

lane

④

boulder

500

400

300

Ross's Camp

shut

×site of Roman tile kilns

lane

⑤

Eskdale

continuation opposite

If starting the walk at Ravenglass —
the Castle car park may be reached
directly by road or, more pleasantly,
by a right of way passing the Roman bath-house
and emerging on the A595 200 yards west of it.
(map below)

railway (mainline)

R. Mite

100

WHITEHALL

A595

continuation on previous page

Castle car park

road

A595

Ravenglass and Eskdale Railway

war memorial

layby

farm

R. Mite

railway stations

car park

private road

public path

gate

R. Esk

Roman Fort

Roman villa or bath house

tarn

Ravenglass

R. Esk

this path branches left on grass from the private road just before a fork

207

18 Scout Scar
from Kendal

Scout Scar offers not just an enjoyable excursion into the fells from Kendal, but the chance to follow quite literally in Wainwright's footsteps.

Kendal was Wainwright's home after he moved to the Lake District from Blackburn in 1941, and it has several reminders of one of its most famous adopted sons. Wainwright worked in the borough treasurer's office at the town hall at the start of this walk for nearly three decades, somehow holding down the full-time job while researching and writing his *Pictorial Guides*. Not far from here, in a passageway housing local businesses – including the Westmorland Gazette newspaper, an early publisher of the guides – is Wainwright's Yard, named in his honour in 2003.

While Scout Scar does not share the height or dramatic location of the fells in the Lake District proper, its airy top and sharp drop to one side make it an exciting place to be. There are fine views all around, and a shelter under which to rest and enjoy your lunch, even when it is pouring with rain. This walk follows Wainwright's suggested circular route up and down Scout Scar – 'A walk above others: a pleasure every step of the way,' as he wrote.

If time is short or you want to skip the steep roadside stretches at the beginning and end, a car and obliging driver to drop you off and pick you up would shorten the total distance. But avoid adding to the traffic if you can, as it is the only downside to this walk – much heavier on the roads in and around Kendal than it was in Wainwright's day, with the hum from the A591 in particular accompanying you for much of the way round – and while the distance is fairly long, the walking throughout is easy. So leave the car, try to ignore the noise of the roads, and do as Wainwright suggested by packing some lunch and making a day of it.

From *The Outlying Fells of Lakeland*

Distance 7½ miles (12km)

Ascent 1,000 feet (305m)

Start and finish point The town hall on Highgate in Kendal (SD 515 926)

Ordnance Survey maps Explorer OL7; Landranger 97

Getting there

Getting near Kendal by car is easy – it is ten minutes from junction 36 of the M6 and well connected by the A591 and A6 too – but the traffic and a baffling one-way system around it will make the last part of your journey the hardest. There is limited free car parking by the river, but this is usually full from mid-morning. Otherwise, try the car park by Abbot Hall on Kirkland as you enter the town from the south, or on Blackhall Road by the shopping centre from the north.

Buses serving Kendal include the 555, connecting it south to Lancaster and north to Keswick and several popular tourist towns and villages in between. The many other services include the 106 from Penrith; 532 and 530 from Cartmel; and X35 from Barrow-in-Furness and other western towns. The bus station is a couple of minutes' walk from the start of this walk, and not much further is the train station, which connects with Oxenholme, the main line gateway to the Lake District, a very short ride away, and runs on to Windermere.

Facilities, food and drink

Kendal has plenty of pubs, restaurants, cafés and shops to stock up on a picnic for a walk, including a branch of Booths supermarket off Wainwright's Yard (015397 42370, www. booths.co.uk). For a well-earned treat at the end of this walk, you could try the 1657 Chocolate House on Branthwaite Brow

(015395 40702, www.chocolatehouse1657.co.uk), where just about everything on offer is made from chocolate. The Quaker Tapestry Tearooms on Stramongate (015397 22975, www. quaker-tapestry.co.uk) and Charlie's Café Bar on Stricklandgate (015397 40898) are two family-friendly places for good light meals and teas, while a short drive south out of town on the A591 is Low Sizergh Barn, a farm that has spawned a good food and craft shop and tearoom, from which children can watch as the cows are brought in to be milked (015395 60426).

The tourist information centre, which used to be housed in the town hall but is now further north in town on Stramongate at the Made in Cumbria shop (015397 35891, www.madeincumbria. co.uk) is the best starting point for information about the many attractions in Kendal and near by. Particularly recommended is the Kendal Museum near the train station – Wainwright was an honorary curator here for thirty years, and there are collections of his original drawings and pages, as well as some of his old walking gear and famous pipe in a recreation of his office. Check opening times in advance as they are now sadly limited (015398 15597, www.kendalmuseum.org.uk). The Abbot Hall gallery and Museum of Lakeland Life, sited together at the other end of town off Kirkland (015397 22464, www.abbothall.org.uk), are also excellent, and have a children's playground close by.

Directions
1 Cross the road from the town hall at the traffic lights to climb up Allhallows Lane, soon becoming Beast Banks. Turn right on to Mount Pleasant, continuing on to Serpentine Road as it swings to the right. Turn right at the T-junction, and after 55 yards (50m) cross the road to turn left on to a path into Serpentine Woods, marked by a signpost. Keep to the right hand edge of the wood as you climb until you reach a gap in the wall, emerging to fine views and Kendal below you to the right. Continue ahead on a clear path with a wall on your left. Pass through a gap in the wall and bear right, soon joining another path with another wall to your right.

2 Continue to pass under Kettlewell Crag, then rise up to a stile by a wall corner. Ahead is Helsfell Nab. Rise up over the ridge on top of this, passing the thirteenth tee of the golf course at the highest point. The grassy path descends, then joins a wall. Follow it to the wall corner then rise up the rough path, the sound of traffic from the A591 getting louder as you do so. At the top, turn left and over a wooden stile to reach a footbridge over the A591 (SD 499 935).

3 Once across the road, cross two wooden stiles in quick succession and then cross the pasture. Reach a stile in a wall corner, and take the right of two signed paths to rise up to the cairn on Cunswick Scar; on a clear day you can see the cairn from the stile. From the cairn, turn sharp left, almost back the way you came, to pick up a path down. It soon joins a wall on your right. When the wall turns right, continue ahead on a farm track (a sign close by indicates Gamblesmire Lane). The track descends to a road by a farm.

4 Turn right up the road, and take care – it is not busy, but there is no pavement and the cars travel fast. Pass a car park on your right, and soon turn left through a gate, marked by a public footpath sign. This very clear path rises up to Scout Scar. Take care with children along the top, as there is no fence between the path and a drop to the right. You soon reach a circular shelter (SD 487 919), nicely restored since Wainwright's day and with a view indicator to help identify the fells.

5 Continue along the escarpment for ¾ mile (1.2km), again taking care with the drop to your right, until you reach a large cairn in a small depression. Here turn left on to the very clear path and walk for 1¼ miles (2km) to a road, crossing one wall over a stile and another through a kissing gate, then a field (this was at one time a racecourse). Turn left down the road to the outskirts of Kendal. At a junction cross straight over, then at the next turn right downhill. You are now back on Beast Banks, which leads steeply down to the town hall.

Scout Scar

visiting
Cunswick Scar 679'
Scout Scar 764'

1000 feet of ascent

from KENDAL TOWN HALL
7½ miles
4 hours
but preferably
take sandwiches
and make a day of it

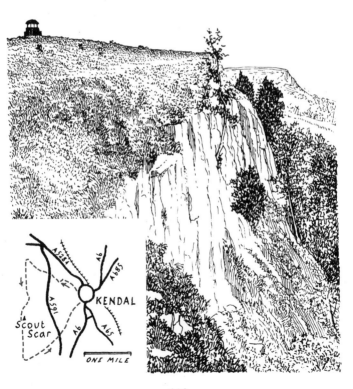

West of Kendal a sloping shelf of limestone rises at an easy gradient for two miles and then suddenly collapses in a long and spectacular cliff, the ground falling away sharply through a fringe of woodlands to the flat pastures of the Lyth Valley, once an inlet of the sea. The effect on the senses of this unexpected convulsion of the landscape is dramatic, even momentarily alarming on a first visit, and no matter how often repeated a slight feeling of shock returns each time as the scene is suddenly confronted. Coming up from Kendal there is nothing to suggest that the next step will not be like the last, but all at once you are on the brink of Scout Scar and ahead is a profound void.

But far below is a picture as fair as any in the country. Richly endowed with noble trees and emerald fields silvered by streams, the scattered white farmsteads of Lyth, renowned for their annual harvest of damsons, each in a surround of blossom, present a springtime scene with charm enough for a hundred canvasses, and in the other seasons of the year, even under snow, which comes but rarely to this sequestered sanctuary, the impression of rural tranquillity is one to lift the heart..... Even Kendal, a quiet country town, seems terribly urban in comparison.

Above this level strath a tangled array of colourful foothills rise inland from the estuary of the Kent against an exciting background: the hills of Lakeland, a rugged skyline of familiar summits, the mountains you once loved to climb. In other directions the panorama is even more extensive: the Howgill Fells are hardly less imposing, while Ingleborough and the Pennines fade into distance. As an all-round viewpoint Scout Scar ranks amongst the very best. Nothing is seen that is not beautiful.

The escarpment and the views are rewards enough, but the walk up from Kendal has merit too. It is on limestone, pure limestone without intrusions of other rocks, and is attended by the joys inherent in limestone: firm dry turf, here interspersed with gorse and juniper, heather and bracken; scree and clints that make tinkling music under the feet, and interesting formations, all allied to glorious views.

Scout Scar has a counterpart to the north, an almost identical twin, in Cunswick Scar: a mile-long, dead-straight escarpment, but curiously set back on another fault-line. In a fracture between the two is a scenic road with a popular car park.

This is a walk above others : a pleasure every step of the way.

In Serpentine Woods

This old summerhouse is passed during the walk through the woods. Inside is a notice board with a map and details of the history and ecology of Serpentine Woods. Note as you emerge on to the fell, in the wall between the gateway and the stile, a memorial tablet to DARWIN LEIGHTON "Friend of all creatures in this wood", whose daily ritual it was to feed the birds and squirrels.

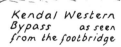

Kendal Western Bypass as seen from the footbridge

At the end of the deep cutting the northbound motorist gets his first near view of the hills.

The cairn on Cunswick Scar, looking to Kentmere

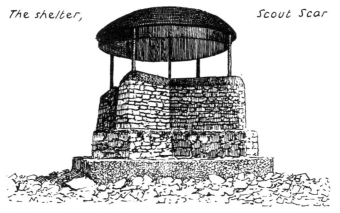

The shelter,   Scout Scar

This well-built shelter, erected in 1912 as a memorial to King George V and restored in 2002, is a conspicuous landmark on the highest part of Scout Scar. On the inside of the dome, and above eye level, is a remarkably clear and accurate view indicator.

The Lakeland skyline from west to north

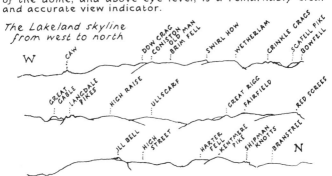

Ponder, as you walk upon Scout Scar, where does all the rain go that falls on this wide upland? The ground is bone dry. There are no streams. Does the rain simply percolate into the limestone and evaporate? Or is there, somewhere beneath the surface, a master cave, an underground lake with no outlet? Nowhere in the vicinity are there any resurgences, and there are no major springs.

The secret is locked in the twin bosoms of Cunswick Scar and Scout Scar. Man has, as yet, no key. (*Note:* one possible explanation is the substantial underground stream that emerges at the back of Kendal Parish Church.)

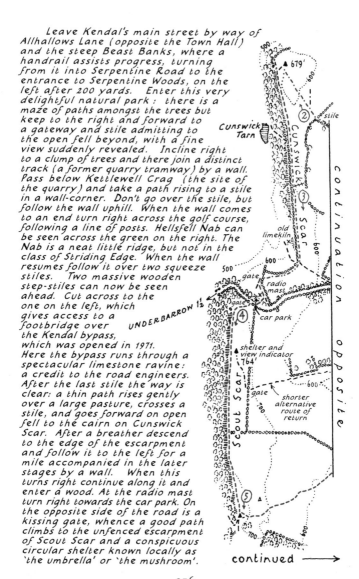

Leave Kendal's main street by way of Allhallows Lane (opposite the Town Hall) and the steep Beast Banks, where a handrail assists progress, turning from it into Serpentine Road to the entrance to Serpentine Woods, on the left after 200 yards. Enter this very delightful natural park: there is a maze of paths amongst the trees but keep to the right and forward to a gateway and stile admitting to the open fell beyond, with a fine view suddenly revealed. Incline right to a clump of trees and there join a distinct track (a former quarry tramway) by a wall. Pass below Kettlewell Crag (the site of the quarry) and take a path rising to a stile in a wall-corner. Don't go over the stile, but follow the wall uphill. When the wall comes to an end turn right across the golf course, following a line of posts. Hellsfell Nab can be seen across the green on the right. The Nab is a neat little ridge, but not in the class of Striding Edge. When the wall resumes follow it over two squeeze stiles. Two massive wooden step-stiles can now be seen ahead. Cut across to the one on the left, which gives access to a footbridge over the Kendal bypass, which was opened in 1971. Here the bypass runs through a spectacular limestone ravine: a credit to the road engineers. After the last stile the way is clear: a thin path rises gently over a large pasture, crosses a stile, and goes forward on open fell to the cairn on Cunswick Scar. After a breather descend to the edge of the escarpment and follow it to the left for a mile accompanied in the later stages by a wall. When this turns right continue along it and enter a wood. At the radio mast turn right towards the car park. On the opposite side of the road is a kissing gate, whence a good path climbs to the unfenced escarpment of Scout Scar and a conspicuous circular shelter known locally as 'the umbrella' or 'the mushroom'.

216

continued →

ONE MILE

If a car is available the initial steep
climb out of Kendal can be avoided
by starting the walk at the top
of the lane along the east side
of Serpentine Woods.

WINDERMERE

Helsfell
(farm)

barn

WINDERMERE

300

400

200

BURNESIDE

River Kent

Helsfell
Nab   stile
stile

① footbridge

Kettlewell
Crag

barn

car
park

SHAP A6

Kendal

Golf
Course

600

Serpentine
Woods

Bus Station

Town Hall

Bank
Head
(farm)

500

former quarries
and lime works

Castle

continuation opposite

Underbarrow
Road

Western

A591

⑦

River Kent

Kendal

Parish Church

500

Bradley Field
(farm)

Brigsteer Road

300

600

cattle
grid
and gate

stile

Bypass

400

⑥   gate

former racecourse

gate

LANCASTER

A6 LANCASTER

SETTLE A65

500

BRIGSTEER 2

continued:
     After a good long rest (no use
     overdoing things) depart from
the shelter and resume the walk along the
escarpment south for almost a mile until, in
a slight depression, a path turns off left at
a cairn and leads distinctly across open fell
to a kissing gate in a wall followed by another (it seems a
little nostalgic to be talking of kissing gates at our age) to
cross a former racecourse and so reach the Brigsteer road
at a stile.   An easy downhill mile along this, passing the
obelisk on the Norman motte of Castle Howe, will return
you to Kendal Town Hall flushed with success.

19 Stickle Pike

from Broughton Mills

Horseshoe walks, on which one traverses the length of one ridge and returns on a second along the other side of a valley, are among the Lake District's classic days out. By their nature they tend to be long, and popular ones like the Fairfield, Langdale and Ennerdale horseshoes are beyond the capabilities of most young families. But this walk provides a perfect introduction to horseshoe walking with superb ridges and views, while clocking in at only a little over 5 miles (8km). There is a considerable amount of climbing along the way for so short a distance, and smaller children may find some of the ascents too much, but there is a handy bail-out point at a road halfway along the route for those who get too tired, marked in the directions. But for children who complete the round, the accumulation of several peaks and the high-rise ridge walking will provide a sense of great achievement.

There is a cluster of summits on each ridge, with Dunnerdale Beck and a road dividing them, and they are great places for children to explore. The walk's flagship fell is Stickle Pike, a peak so spectacularly shaped that it feels much higher and more daunting than it actually is – a mini-Matterhorn that can be reached by most children within a few hours. Apart from a scramble up Stickle Pike and some old quarry paths just after the turn of the horseshoe, the walking underfoot is generally straightforward, and the scenery very diverse for a relatively short distance. A bonus for parents is The Blacksmith Arms close to the starting point in Broughton Mills, one of the very best pubs in the Lake District.

From *The Outlying Fells of Lakeland*

Distance 5½ miles (9km)

Ascent 1,700 feet (520m)

Start and finish point The bridge over the River Lickle at Broughton Mills (SD 222 907)

Ordnance Survey maps Explorer OL6; Landranger 96

Getting there

Broughton Mills is about 2 miles (3.2km) north of Broughton, which is just off the A595. Follow the A593 out of Broughton towards Torver and Coniston, then leave it to the left just over a mile later at the signpost for Broughton Mills. There is parking for a few cars on the lay-bys either side of the bridge. If these are full, you may be able to park at the Blacksmiths Arms up the hill from the pub if you are visiting it before or after the walk; tell the staff at the pub your plans. Turn left from the pub to reach the bridge.

This is one of only a few walks in this book not easily accessible by public transport. The nearest you can get is Broughton, which is served by the number 7 bus between Barrow-in-Furness and Millom, and the 511 from Ulverston, though this runs on Tuesdays and Thursdays only. Broughton in turn is 2 miles (3.2km) from Foxfield station on the coastal line.

Facilities, food and drink

The Blacksmiths Arms, a short walk up the hill from the walk's starting point, is a centuries-old inn that is full of character, with oak-beamed ceilings and corridors, slate floors, open fires and several cosy side rooms. It serves good food and beer and welcomes children (01229 716824, www.theblacksmithsarms.com).

Broughton has more facilities including, on the lovely square, the Manor Arms pub (01229 716286, www.manorarmsthesquare.co.uk) and a restaurant, Beswicks (01229 716285, www.beswicks.co.uk). The Broughton Village Bakery and Café on Princes Street (01229 716284, www.broughtonvillagebakery.co.uk) is outstanding and will make up packed lunches for the fells; phone your order ahead to pick up on the way through.

Directions

1 From the bridge, take the narrow road with a road sign indicating no through way. It rises up to Green Bank Farm. Here, bend to the right on a rougher track, indicated by two public bridleway signposts for the Duddon valley. This soon leads past a white cottage and turns into a thin footpath into the wood ahead. With a wall on your left, the path leads up to the top of the wood, leaving it through a wooden gate. Rise up the grassy slopes ahead, soon approaching a picnic table. The path bends left here and contours the hillside, mostly with walls on either side and fine views of the rolling hills and the Duddon estuary to the left. Later on it passes through two gates, the first just after crossing a stream and the second after passing a barn to your left (SD 213 912).

2 The fell ahead of you after this gate is Hovel Knott. Do not take the thin path up through the bracken, but instead follow the path around its base, with a wall on your left. Where the walls falls away to the left, continue ahead on the path through the bracken. After rising up, the grassy path meets three clear forks in short succession; turn right at the first two and left at the third. The path continues to rise, with Little Stickle on your right. At the end of a marshy area to your left, bear right on another fork to climb up to the ridge. If you want to add Great Stickle to your bag of peaks, detour right to the top, which is marked by an Ordnance Survey triangulation point and cairn (SD 212 916).

3 Back on the ridge, the conical fell of Stickle Pike should be visible ahead. The path makes directly for it, soon weaving past tarns on Tarn Hill, then dropping down to a depression. Take the right-hand of the two paths ahead at the grassy crossroads here, then rise and drop to another, marshy, depression. The path now leads you steeply up to the right of Stickle Pike. At a col, by a cairn and some jagged rocks, divert left up to the top of Stickle Pike; it is not far, but a bit of a scramble in places. For a slightly easier way up, continue along the col for about 55 yards (50m) to another cairn, and turn left up it there. The summit is a spectacular array of jagged rocks, and the highest point is marked by a cairn precariously balanced on one of them (SD 212 928).

4 Walk carefully back down from the summit to the path and continue along it, soon glimpsing Stickle Tarn to your right. The grassy path forks into two soon after it; take the left-hand one and soon emerge at a road (SD 215 933). There are spaces to park here, so it makes a good pick-up point for anyone with access to an obliging driver. If you want to keep walking but cut out the climbing that lies ahead, turn right down the road, which leads for about 2 miles (3.2km) all the way back to the bridge at Broughton Mills.

5 To continue on to the return leg of the horseshoe, cross the road and bear half right to pick up a path, signposted as a public bridleway for Seathwaite. At the first fork, bear left to curve around the rocks and slate, then leave the path to the right to walk around the other side, and leave that to the left to climb up to the spoil heaps ahead. The path weaves in and out of these; take care with children here, as the slate can be slippery and there are drops and old mine openings off the path. At the top mine hole, bear half right on a path up to the ridge ahead, then bear right along it. The path is mostly good, but faint in a few places, though the way along the ridge, heading south, should be clear. It crosses a couple of heights marked by cairns, but then bends to the left of Raven's Crag to avoid the tricky descent on the other side. After this, the broad grassy slopes of The Knott are in view, with a large cairn on top. Descend to the depression in front of it, then make one last climb up to the cairn (SD 224 919).

6 After stopping to look back on the horseshoe, descend from The Knott. There are several paths down, but the ones over grass rather than bracken are best. At the bottom, look for the gate and stile in the wall, leading on to the road (SD 225 914). Turn right along it. The road winds down towards Broughton Mills, bending left at a junction, passing a church, and arriving back at the bridge.

Stickle Pike

visiting
  Great Stickle, 1001'
  Tarn Hill, 1020'
  Stickle Pike, 1231'
  a nameless summit, 1183'
  The Knott, 925'

1700 feet of ascent

from BROUGHTON MILLS

5¼ miles

5 hours

This walk may be
described as
"The Dunnerdale
Horseshoe"
*(bearing in mind
the note below)*

*from the
south*

Dunnerdale, to most Lakeland visitors, is the valley of the River Duddon, this being the name of the parish, but the true Dunnerdale is, geographically, a side-valley of the River Lickle two miles in length and watered by Dunnerdale Beck, quite independent of the Duddon. Nor should Stickle Pike and Stickle Tarn, referred to in this chapter, be confused with places of like name in Langdale — they are a day's march away.

The Dunnerdale Fells are low in stature, small in extent and insignificant on the map, yet they assert themselves on the local landscape in a bristly defiance of accepted mountain standards. Of course they are not worthy of comparison with Scafell or Great Gable, but they refuse to admit it. Where else in Lakeland is there so rugged a skyline? Where else, outside Skye, is there an array of peaks so crowded? Well, there is something in their claim. Here, certainly, is an upland tormented by a confusion of crags and peaked outcrops: all in miniature, amounting to nothing, really, in the general lie of the land, but with a magnetism that compels the eye and challenges the feet. Picnic parties by the lower Duddon notice the pugnacious, rather impudent beginning of the group in the sharp rocky turrets rising out of steep bracken slopes; walkers in the valley of the Lickle see their eastern aspect as a serrated skyline of abrupt upsurges and downfalls, a chaotic jumble of mini-summits.

The kingpin of this area is Stickle Pike, a mere 1231 feet above the sea yet a budding Matterhorn with many juvenile satellites.... But it is all make-believe, really, all pretence. To do the round of the ridges is actually quite simple. The aggressive appearance from below is belied on acquaintance ..... there are no dragons on these tops, no menace in their rocks. Instead there are lovely tarns where asphodel and cotton grass and bogbean colour the shallow waters, adding gaiety to the scene and scenting the air, lichened boulders bright with parsley fern, soft carpets of turf and bracken, innumerable pleasant couches where one can lie in comfort and think of real fells like Scafell and Great Gable. But do not voice these thoughts: Stickle Pike is proud and easily hurt.

Stickle Pike
from
Great Stickle

Some walks have obvious beginnings and follow so natural a line that directions are not really necessary. This one is not in that category. It is not easy to see, at Broughton Mills, how to get a footing on either of the two ridges that rise from the maze of woodlands and walled fields above the hamlet, nor at this distance to identify precisely the fells peeping over the trees. Only the Knott is clearly in view.

However, the thing to do is to get started correctly, and, over the bridge across the Lickle, a tarmac lane with a NO THROUGH ROAD sign points the way to go. There is no further guidance by signs, here or beyond. At the first farm, Green Bank, do not enter the farmyard, but take a lane uphill as far as a cottage, opposite which a thin and stony track winds up into a wood with a wall on the left. Escape at a gate from the clutches of foliage and continue ahead, passing a picnic table with a beautiful view, and bearing left into a lane, which contours the slope, rising and falling slightly, and reaches the open fell at the second of two gates, above a barn. The shapely Hovel Knott appears ahead : contour around its base, still on a path, and ascend its far slope of bracken, where walls are left behind. Bear right at the first fork, right at the second fork and left at the third fork. Little Stickle is now close on the right. At the end of a marshy area bear right to the ridge, where a detour to the right leads to the Ordnance column (S.5453) on the abrupt summit of Great Stickle. The main objective, Stickle Pike, is now in view to the north. Reach it by keeping to the indefinite ridge over the well-named Tarn Hill to the depression below the sharp rise to the Pike. After passing a fenced marsh the path heads in the wrong direction; cut across to a clear path, bearing right to avoid the bracken if necessary. Don't tackle Stickle Pike directly up its steep front but follow the clear path to a col on its east side, from which an indistinct path climbs steeply left and joins the main path to the summit, which is a fine vantage point. Having got your wind back, go down by the main path, joining a wide grass path that passes near to Stickle Tarn on its gentle descent to the top of the road now in sight ahead. (This path is obviously the tourist route to the Pike from cars parked on the verge). The road links Broughton Mills and the Duddon Valley, and provides a quick way back to the starting point (right not left) if your legs are buckling. Those who are damned if they will give in should cross the tarmac to a path going forward to the extensive Stainton Ground Quarries and ascend amongst the spoil heaps to the topmost hole. A slanting course half-right now climbs easily to the second of the walk's two ridges (and the least interesting). Go along this to the right, over point 1183' but skirting Raven's Crag to the left and descend to a depression beyond which is a simple walk to the big cairn on the Knott. Take a last look round (most of the route is visible from here), then descend due south, keeping to grass rather than bracken, and, with the farm of Knott End well to your right, reach a gate at the foot of the slope giving access to a tarmac road, which follow downhill, joining the valley road, passing the church and so returning to Broughton Mills pleased with yourself. A very good performance, considering your age.

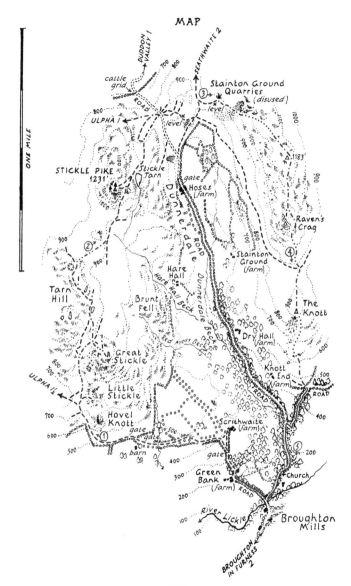

MAP

ONE MILE

DUDDON VALLEY 1

SEATHWAITE 2

cattle grid

700 800

900

ROAD

ULPHA 1

800

level

Stainton Ground Quarries (disused)

③ level

1000

1100

1000

STICKLE PIKE 1231

Stickle Tarn

gate

Hoses (farm)

△ 1183

900

1000

Dunnerdale ROAD

②

900

Raven's Crag △

Stainton Ground (farm)

④

Tarn Hill

Hare Hall

Hare Hall Beck

Brunt Fell

Dunnerdale Beck

The Knott △

Red Moss Beck

Dry Hall (farm)

Great Stickle

ULPHA 1½

700

Little Stickle

Knott End (farm)

500 ROAD

ROAD

400

Hovel Knott

600

gate

gate

500

①

barn

400

Scrithwaite (farm)

⑤ 200

Church

gate

Green Bank (farm) ROAD

300

200

100

River Lickle

Broughton Mills

100

BROUGHTON IN FURNESS 2

225

Stickle Pike

Mountain summits are
especially attractive
when they are rocky,
abrupt on all sides,
small in extent and
exciting. These are
attributes in which
Stickle Pike's top
scores over those
of many a higher
and better-known
fell. It has also
the added appeal
of a shapely
cairn on a
natural
plinth:
a rock
outcrop
on the
highest
point.

A second cairn occupies the south end of the short and
undulating ridge forming the summit, but this is very
inferior to the main cairn.

The view is good within the limitations imposed by the
modest altitude. The high skyline of the Pillar, Scafell,
Bowfell and Coniston groups forms an effective horizon
to the north but much of the detail of these mountains
is obstructed by the nearer Harter Fell and Caw, which
stand like sentinels above the lovely Duddon Valley. In
other directions the scenes are mainly coastal with the
estuary and lower reaches of the Duddon, backed by a
full-length Black Combe range, intimately prominent.

Further left is a glimpse of Morecambe Bay.

Near the beginning
of the walk —
Hovel Knott

Near the end of the walk —
*Cairn on The Knott,
looking to Raven's Crag and Caw*

20 Harter Fell
from Eskdale

Harter Fell is the highest peak in this book, and this its most testing walk – suitable for families with plenty of stamina and some good walking already behind them. For those who are up to the challenge, the walk combines an ascent of Harter Fell with a detour on the way back to Eskdale to see the remains of the spectacularly situated Roman fort of Hardknott Castle.

Other fells in this book are all below 2,000 feet (610m), and many of them less than half that. But Harter Fell, at 2,140 feet or just over 650m, qualifies because if offers families a challenging but achievable climb from one of the most attractive valleys in the Lake District. 'Not many fells can be described as beautiful,' writes Wainwright. 'But the word fits Harter Fell.' As he adds, it is a fell that is as good to climb as it is to look at, with the steady ascent rewarded with a dramatic, craggy top and wide-reaching views over fells, valleys and lakes. 'There is not a more charming ascent than this, which is a delight from start to finish.'

The way back down skirts past Dunnerdale Forest before reaching the Hardknott Pass, from which the Castle makes a very worthwhile diversion, especially for children interested in Roman history. It was founded by Hadrian in the second century along the road between forts at Ravenglass and Ambleside, but fell out of use from the late fourth century. There are plenty of remains to see, including of the headquarters and bathhouse, while the nearby parade ground is easily spotted.

From *Book Four: The Southern Fells*

Distance 7½ miles (12km)

Ascent 2,000 feet (610m)

Start and finish point The Woolpack Inn near Boot in Eskdale (NY 191 010).

Ordnance Survey maps Explorer OL6; Landranger 90 and 96

Getting there

The Woolpack is about 1 mile (1.6km) east of Boot in the Eskdale valley. If you visit before or after the walk you may be able to park in front of the inn; tell the staff your plans. Otherwise there is parking either back in Boot or at the foot of the Hardknott Pass (NY 212 011); parking at the latter shortens the end of this walk and can be a starting point for an ascent of Harter Fell to reduce the distance further. Eskdale is best reached from the west; you can come from the east over the Hardknott and Wrynose Passes, though they are not advised in bad weather or the dark or for anyone who feels poorly along winding roads.

The walk can be accessed by the Ravenglass and Eskdale railway, which runs from Ravenglass – which in turn connects with the Cumbrian coast line – to the pretty Dalegarth station in Boot (01229 717171, www.ravenglass-railway.co.uk). Turn left out of the station along the road for 1½ miles (2.4km) up to the starting point at the Woolpack.

Facilities, food and drink

The Woolpack Inn and its adjacent Hardknott Bar and Café serve excellent food, local beers and tea and coffee, and will make up packed lunches for fellwalkers (019467 23230, www.woolpack.co.uk). Children are very welcome, and there is a small room with toys and games to keep them entertained. The Woolpack is also a great place to stay, and at the time of writing it had plans to launch the Hardknott Shop selling toys and games as well as local produce and crafts.

Boot has two more good eating pubs in the Boot Inn (019467 23224, www.bootinn.co.uk) and the Brook House Inn (019467 23288, www.brookhouseinn.co.uk). Dalegarth station has a family-friendly café as well as a visitor centre, gift shop and adventure playground for children.

Directions

1 Turn right along the road from the Woolpack Inn. After nearly 220 yards (200m), cross and turn left by a sign for Penny Hill Farm on to a lane. It drops down to the River Esk, then crosses it over a lovely old bridge (Doctor Bridge). Continue ahead, marked by a public bridleway sign for Penny Hill. The track now leads up to the farm, with Harter Fell looming in front of you. Just before the farm, leave the path to the right via a wooden gate, the way indicated by a permitted path sign for Harter Fell, Jubilee Bridge and Hardknott. Cross the field with a wall to your left to another gate, then turn left, following the white arrows to another gate and, after dropping down to the main farm track, another one. The track continues through farmland and gets near the Esk again. The river remains in sight and sound as you continue.

2 About ½ mile (800m) from the farm, enter a small wood at a wooden gate and continue ahead, very soon crossing a stream coming down the fellside. About 30 yards (30m) after that, ignore the public bridleway that forks left through a gap in the wall, and continue along the footpath. In another 110 yards (100m), cross another stream via a footbridge and pass through a wooden gate (NY 204 006).

3 The path now rises steeply up, with a wall, soon replaced by a fence, on your right, and a stream the other side of it. Cross a stile and, further on, reach a gate in wall. Go through and look back for majestic views of Eskdale. The path beyond the gate climbs again. Where it levels out, take a fainter, grassier path off to the left, aiming just to the right of the craggy peak up ahead. This path skirts past Birker Fell and continues to climb until it reaches a junction of paths by a small cairn. Turn left here and climb again to the top of Harter Fell; a side path to the left leads a few metres up to an Ordnance Survey cairn (SD 218 997). The true summit is among the slightly taller rocky outcrops near by, though the cairn is close enough for most walkers.

4 Drop back down to the main path, and continue along it heading east; do not take the right-hand fork that bears south. The northern end of Dunnerdale Forest soon appears down below. The path here is indistinct in places, and care is needed as the grassy slopes can be slippery and boggy, but continue to aim for the far left tip of the forest and you will be on the right track. Further down the path crosses a stile in a fence and continues, with the fence on your right, to another. Soon after this the fence turns sharply right, but continue ahead, through a gap in a broken wall and over the outcrop ahead. Continue on and emerge at a road – the Hardknott Pass (NY 229 015). If you are unsure about the path here, head due north and you will soon hit the road.

5 Turn left along the road. After about ¼ mile (400m), at a hairpin bend to the left, leave it to the right, the way indicated by a public footpath signpost. The path stays near the road at first but then bends away from it to pass the spectacular ruin of Hardknott Castle to the right, before bending back down to the road (NY 216 012).

6 Turn right down the road, cutting off the hairpin bends that the drivers have to tackle by taking the side-paths across them. Pass a car parking place – a good pick-up point for any tired walkers – and immediately before a cattle grid leave the road to the left, in the direction of a public bridleway signpost. Cross a stream over a fine old bridge (Jubilee Bridge) and climb up to two wooden gates in quick succession. Once through them, do not take the broad grassy path ahead but stay on one by the wall. Keep it on your right, then climb slightly to another wooden gate in a cross-wall. Go through and follow the path ahead to another gate, leading into a wooded area and, soon, another gate. The gate after this is the one from which you started climbing earlier. Retrace your steps by continuing over the footbridge and fields back to Penny Hill Farm, not forgetting the diversion around the farmyard. Back in front of the farm, turn left up the track, over Doctor Bridge and up to the road, then turn right for the Woolpack Inn.

Harter Fell

2140'

from Penny Hill

Birks Bridge

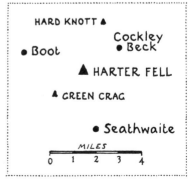

HARD KNOTT ▲

● Boot

Cockley
● Beck

▲ HARTER FELL

▲ GREEN CRAG

● Seathwaite

MILES

0   1   2   3   4

NATURAL FEATURES

Not many fells can be described as *beautiful*, but the word fits Harter Fell, especially so when viewed from Eskdale. The lower slopes on this flank climb steeply from the tree-lined curves of the River Esk in a luxurious covering of bracken, higher is a wide belt of heather, and finally spring grey turrets and ramparts of rock to a neat and shapely pyramid. The Duddon slopes are now extensively planted, and here too, thanks to the good taste of the Forestry Commission in this area, deciduous trees and evergreens amongst the crags will, in due course, make a colourful picture.

The fell is not only good to look at, but good to climb, interest being well sustained throughout and reaching a climax in the last few feet, an upthrust of naked rock where the walker must turn cragsman if he is to enjoy the magnificent panorama from the uttermost point.

Harter Fell rises between the mid-valleys of the Esk and the Duddon, not at the head, and is therefore not the source of either river although it feeds both.

The head of Eskdale, from the summit of Harter Fell

MAP

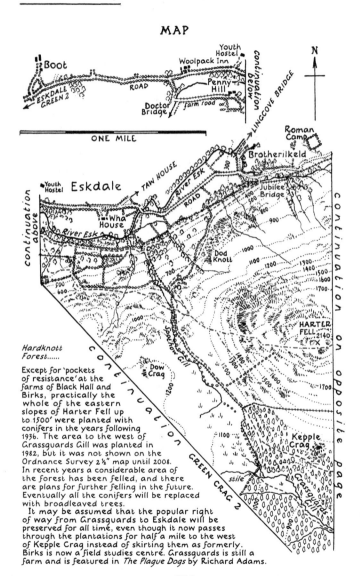

Hardknott Forest......

Except for 'pockets of resistance' at the farms of Black Hall and Birks, practically the whole of the eastern slopes of Harter Fell up to 1500' were planted with conifers in the years following 1936. The area to the west of Grassguards Gill was planted in 1982, but it was not shown on the Ordnance Survey 2½" map until 2008. In recent years a considerable area of the forest has been felled, and there are plans for further felling in the future. Eventually all the conifers will be replaced with broadleaved trees.

It may be assumed that the popular right of way from Grassguards to Eskdale will be preserved for all time, even though it now passes through the plantations for half a mile to the west of Kepple Crag instead of skirting them as formerly. Birks is now a field studies centre. Grassguards is still a farm and is featured in *The Plague Dogs* by Richard Adams.

234

MAP

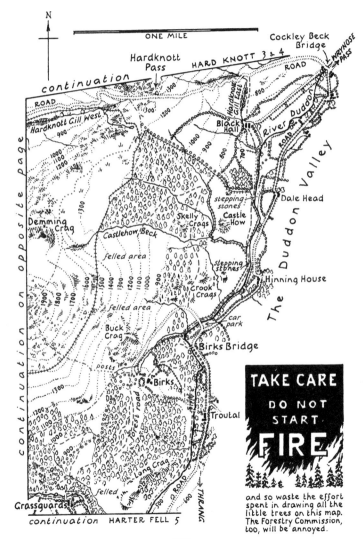

N

ONE MILE

Cockley Beck Bridge

WRYNOSE PASS

Hardknott Pass

HARD KNOTT 3 & 4 ROAD

continuation

ROAD

Hardknott Gill West

Hardknott Gill East

Black Hall

River Duddon

ROAD

900
1000
1100
1200

1300

1300
1200

1300

900
600
700
800
600
700

Demming Crag

Castlehow Beck

Skelly Crags

Castle How

stepping stones

Dale Head

felled area

600
1500
1400
1300
1100
900

1000

stepping stones

Crook Craags

Hinning House

1900
1800
1700

felled area

Buck Crag

car park

The Duddon Valley

1300

posts

Birks Bridge

forest road

Birks

1200
1100
1000
900
800

Troutal

felled

Lang Crag

500
600

Grassguards

continuation

THRANG

ROAD

HARTER FELL 5

continuation on opposite page

TAKE CARE
DO NOT START
FIRE

and so waste the effort spent in drawing all the little trees on this map. The Forestry Commission, too, will be annoyed.

235

MAP

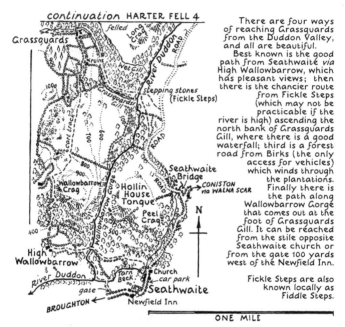

continuation HARTER FELL 4

Grassguards

felled
Long Crag
ruins
River Duddon ROAD
Wet Gill
1000
Grassguards Gill
stepping stones
(Fickle Steps)
Carl Crag
100
900
800
ROAD
Wallowbarrow Crag
Seathwaite Bridge
Hollin House Tongue
CONISTON via WALNA SCAR
Wallowbarrow Gorge
Peel Crag
N
400
500
High Wallowbarrow
River Duddon
Tarn Beck
Church car park
gate
Seathwaite
BROUGHTON
Newfield Inn

ONE MILE

There are four ways of reaching Grassguards from the Duddon Valley, and all are beautiful.

Best known is the good path from Seathwaite via High Wallowbarrow, which has pleasant views; then there is the chancier route from Fickle Steps (which may not be practicable if the river is high) ascending the north bank of Grassguards Gill, where there is a good waterfall; third is a forest road from Birks (the only access for vehicles) which winds through the plantations. Finally there is the path along Wallowbarrow Gorge that comes out at the foot of Grassguards Gill. It can be reached from the stile opposite Seathwaite church or from the gate 100 yards west of the Newfield Inn.

Fickle Steps are also known locally as Fiddle Steps.

Grassguards Gill forms the southern boundary of Harter Fell, but the map has been extended in that direction to include the approaches from Seathwaite.

Harter Fell
from the Walna Scar path

ASCENT FROM ESKDALE
2000 feet of ascent · 3½ miles from Boot

On the approach *via* Penny Hill, doubts will arise in the little tangle of rough country in the vicinity of Spothow Gill, above the walls of the enclosures, where footsteps will tend to gravitate in error to the path going across into the Duddon Valley. It is better to use the path from Jubilee Bridge.

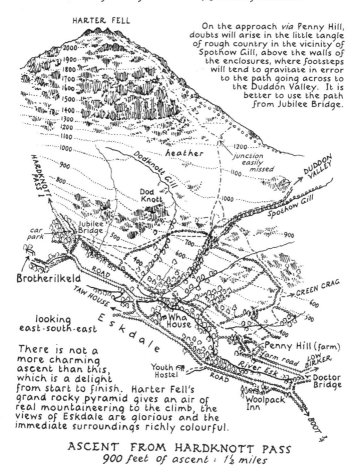

HARTER FELL

looking east-south-east

There is not a more charming ascent than this, which is a delight from start to finish. Harter Fell's grand rocky pyramid gives an air of real mountaineering to the climb, the views of Eskdale are glorious and the immediate surroundings richly colourful.

ASCENT FROM HARDKNOTT PASS
900 feet of ascent · 1½ miles

Little can be said in favour of the obvious route along the swampy ridge from the top of Hardknott Pass, which is pathless for much of its length and lacking in interest. The path leaves the road 200 yards west of the pass. Keep left of the conspicuous Demming Crag.

ASCENT FROM THE DUDDON VALLEY

There is no longer free and open access to the fellside from the Duddon because of the plantations. The summit may be reached from the time-honoured route to Eskdale from Grassguards or by a shorter route starting at Birks Bridge. The route to Birks for vehicles now starts at the car park, and the former drive to Birks from Birks Bridge has become a footpath. Above Birks the route is marked by red-topped posts, which are difficult to follow. Here the route is steep and loose, but it becomes easier when the former plantations are left behind. If the Grassguards Gill route is used it is best to follow the broken wall up to the right from the top of the pass to avoid the considerable descent and ascent involved in keeping to the path.

THE SUMMIT

The true summit from the 'official'

An Ordnance Survey triangulation column gives an air of authenticity to the craggy rise it occupies, but this is clearly not the highest point. Near at hand, east, is a steep-sided outcrop extending several feet nearer to heaven, and beyond that is another, similar but of lower elevation. The middle one of these three rocky tors is therefore the true summit, although it carries no decorations; at first glance it looks unassailable but an investigation on its east side discloses there a breach: the crest may then be reached by simple climbing. The third turret also offers, on its south edge, an easy access to its top. All told, this is a grand and entertaining summit, a place one is loth to leave.

DESCENTS: Crags are continuous along the north edge of the fell and scattered elsewhere, so that the path going down to Eskdale, which is fortunately distinct enough to be found and followed in mist, should be adhered to closely. For the Duddon Valley it is best to use the path to Birks.

1 : 'official' summit
2 : true summit

THE VIEW

Having exercised himself by scrambling up and down the three summits, the visitor can settle himself on the sharp arete of the highest and enjoy a most excellent view. The Scafell group and Upper Eskdale dominate the scene, appearing not quite in such detail as when surveyed from Hard Knott but in better balance —added distance often adds quality to a picture. Over Wrynose Pass there is an array of faraway fells in the Kirkstone area, which will not surprise walkers familiar with that district, where Harter Fell often pops into the views therefrom. Near at hand, east, the Coniston fells bulk largely but unattractively. Lower Eskdale and the Duddon Valley lead the eye to golden sands and glittering sea.

Principal Fells

Look particularly for the Roman fort at Hardknott, of which there is an aerial view.

Lakes and Tarns
ESE : Seathwaite Tarn
WSW : Devoke Water
WNW : Blea Tarn
NW : Eel Tarn
NNW : Burnmoor Tarn

RIDGE ROUTES

There is no defined ridge seawards, although it is possible to keep to the height of land for a dozen miles without (except at one point) descending below 1000ʹ. Northeast, a high ridge continues to Hard Knott and at its lowest depression is crossed by a motor road (Hardknott Pass), from whence the route onwards has been described as a separate ascent (see page Hard Knott 5).

Main entries are in **bold**